INTER
POLITICS

and the

DEMAND

for

GLOBAL
JUSTICE

INTERNATIONAL POLITICS

and the

DEMAND

for

GLOBAL
JUSTICE

James W. Skillen

G.R. WELCH COMPANY, LIMITED
Burlington, Ontario, Canada

DORDT COLLEGE PRESS
Sioux Center, Iowa, U.S.A.

ISBN: 0-919532-84-5

© 1981 by James W. Skillen

G.R. Welch Company, Limited
960 Gateway
Burlington, Ontario
Canada   L7L 5K7

Dordt College Press
Sioux Center, Iowa
U.S.A.   51250

Printed in Canada

To my sister Susannah and brothers
David and John for helping to enlarge
my horizons and encouraging me to
serve the King.

Acknowledgments

With grateful appreciation I wish to thank several friends and colleagues for their help and encouragement in this project. Much of the thinking behind the words came from discussions within the circles of the Association for Public Justice. My colleagues in this Association, especially Rockne McCarthy, William Harper, and Theodore Malloch, were most helpful.

Several colleagues at Dordt College, especially John Hulst and Bernard J. Haan, encouraged me to have this book published.

Paul Schrotenboer published some earlier versions of some parts of the text in the *International Reformed Bulletin* when he was its editor.

Students in my courses on international politics provided much help through their questions, papers, and enthusiasm.

Jack Vanden Berg provided excellent editorial assistance, helping to correct and sharpen my first efforts.

Close friends and family always seem to do the most, even when they are not directly involved in the writing. Doreen, Jeanene, and Jamie provide sustaining love at home.

Contents

Preface

International affairs are no longer the private domain of foreign diplomats. Grain sales or embargoes vitally concern farmers. Auto imports or exports affect a large portion of the labor force. The politics of energy push every country into unwelcome corners of the global village. The threat of nuclear war hangs over the head of every citizen. Whether or not we are prepared to think about the complexities of international relations, those relations are already forcing us to change our lifestyles in dozens of ways.

Opening ourselves to a consideration of global politics, however, can be discouraging and dangerous; the issues are so diverse and complex that we could become lost and confused trying to understand them. Since special expertise is required to handle many of the legal, economic, technical, and military issues, it is possible for zealous amateurs, whether ordinary citizens or government officials, to give bad advice or to influence policymaking negatively. Yet we cannot simply close ourselves off from the rapidly changing world with the hope that events by themselves might produce happy consequences without any demands upon our responsibility. We must not avoid asking the questions, "Where are we?", "What should we do?" and "What responsibilities do we have in the global politics of today?" All of us must ask these questions.

The purpose of this book is to help in formulating those questions. The book is not a collection of solutions for policymakers. It is not a problem-solving encyclopedia encompassing all of today's global issues. It does not try to predict the date when World War III will begin, nor does it attempt to show how we can escape the energy crisis or the arms race in several simple steps.

One of the basic assumptions supporting the arguments of the following chapters is that we can understand our world only if we are willing to step back a bit from all the pressing, pragmatic predicaments in which we find ourselves, in order to see them in a larger light, in a broader context. But step back to where? See the world in what kind of light? What broader context exists? These are the kinds of questions we will try to answer.

The book has been written for all who are concerned about international politics, but especially for college students who might find it helpful as a supplemental text for courses in international relations. Chapters 4 and 5 particularly have students in mind. However, most students of global politics do not sit in college classrooms, and those who make government policy or who report and analyze international events in the media should consider whether the outlook on world politics presented in the following pages opens up something new for them. Could a different angle of vision help the responsible adviser, journalist or official to produce better advice, analyses or policies?

Education and reeducation that will allow us to understand the world in which we live is a greater and greater challenge. There seems to be too much information to digest in too short a time, but the problem is not simply the quantity. The most fundamental question is: "What framework, what perspective, what world view will allow us to understand our world rightly and truthfully?"

Hearing the cry for justice from around the world has motivated this quest for a truthful understanding of the world.

1

Power vs Justice: The Crisis in International Politics

To understand the political character of the age in which we live, it is helpful to glance back over history and consider how the world was understood by people who lived in other eras. What we experience and have come to accept in the modern world is a political order or disorder of separate, independent states relating to each other in a power-political way, for the present framework of international politics has become familiar and acceptable to us only during the last two centuries. But just as this "new" international order is finally becoming familiar to us, it is already revealing its own problems and failures. Thus a brief backward glance may help us look toward the future with greater wisdom and understanding.

Ancient China

If we had been a part of the Chinese Empire in its growth and development from before the time of Christ until recently, we would have lived with a picture of a *single* world with a *single* center, a center which was the Middle Kingdom (China). At the center of the Middle Kingdom ruled the Son

13

of Heaven by authority of the Mandate of Heaven. The Son of Heaven represented the power from on high and cosmic authority of heaven. His rule over this world put the whole world in harmony with what was beyond or above it. And the idea of the world as a single entity had meaning, not in terms of numerous independent states relating to each other in a field of international power relations, but in terms of the Middle Kingdom's central authority within the world. The Middle Kingdom expected that various nations and peoples of the world would gradually come to recognize China as the center of things. These nations would come and bow before the Son of Heaven and thereby begin to participate in the only meaningful civilization in the world. Those who did not recognize the true world with its true center did not have to be evangelized or conquered as if it were absolutely necessary for them to enter the sphere of the Middle Kingdom. Such blind ones could simply be ignored as if they did not exist. Only one world truly existed, the world ordered by the Son of Heaven under the Mandate of Heaven.[1]

Roman Empire

When we turn to look at the ancient Roman Empire we notice a different kind of world order. The Roman Empire arose in the Mediterranean context with another idea of a single world. Here was the Graeco-Roman civilization that defined that *one* true world. If we had been a part of this, we would have assumed that anything beyond our borders was barbarian; it was outside the pale of the world's only true civilization. Unlike China, however, Rome was zealous for imperialistic conquest because the people who lived beyond the empire simply *had* to be brought into the Roman ordering of the world. Barbarians had to be civilized in order that the whole world could be truly unified; the blind or ignorant ought not to be left in their darkness. The Roman emperors had also absorbed a sense of order for this world that derived from a higher ordination—not altogether unlike the Son of

Heaven's relationship to the Mandate of Heaven. The claim of divinity or at least of divine ordination on the part of the Roman emperors was crucial, for it connected the order of this *one* world with the unified harmony on high. Thus the authority of the emperor over this world was connected with the conviction that a superior transcendent authority existed. Bringing the whole world under Roman dominion, then, meant bringing it under the one true order that ought to hold for this one world.[2]

The Holy Roman Empire

If we look at what happened after the Church began to influence the Roman world, we will notice the problematic adoption of Christianity by the Emperor Constantine in the fourth century after Christ. This decision played a part in the Church's eventual adoption of the Roman imperial conception of world order. As the Roman imperial idea was absorbed by the Church, the conviction grew that earthly political order, the order of the Roman Mediterranean world, could only have its true meaning when placed in a proper relationship to the Church. Political order would have to be approved, blessed, and held accountable by those who possessed the keys to the Kingdom—by those institutions which originally received the sword of earthly order from God. During the Middle Ages the "two swords" doctrine was developed, teaching that the Church had received both the spiritual sword and the temporal sword of God's authority over the world. The Church was responsible for granting the sword of earthly political order to kings, to the feudal lords, or to the emperor, while it retained for itself the spiritual sword. Had we lived in the High Middle Ages we would also have had a picture of a single world, of one true civilization, in so far as it was ordered under the gracious auspices of the Church.[3]

These three views of world order are quite different from the view that rules our era. The Chinese idea of the Middle Kingdom which we might describe as the world organized by the Son of Heaven under the Mandate of Heaven; the Roman Empire organized to gain unified mastery over all peoples; the Christian Roman Empire that organized the natural political world under the authority of the one true God by means of the one true Church—these three visions of the world did not allow for a multi-centered world. They did not accept as legitimate a politically-divided world which would then have to achieve political balance through cooperative or uncooperative power plays among separately organized political entities. All three were orders that allowed for only one center, one focus, one dispensation of grace.

Emergence of the Modern State

But about the time of Machiavelli, a significant change began to unfold in the West. Machiavelli lived in what is now Italy at the end of the fifteenth century and the early sixteenth century. Through him, Europeans began to get a picture of politics as an arena or field of pure "power." Political life would have its identity purely in terms of the organization of force. In Machiavelli's view, politics were primarily a matter of the control of power, and from that point of departure the Western world got its conception of the state and of the relations among states that we still use today.

We talk, for example, of the international world as a field where many powers compete with one another—big powers, little powers, middle powers, and superpowers. But if we had spoken this way in ancient China, or in the Roman world, or in the Holy Roman Empire, it would not have made sense, because power simply did not stand by itself in those civilizations, and it certainly could not be legitimately splintered into many separate parts. The power involved in organizing the world, the power of force which had to be used in those ancient systems, always had to be seen in the context of the proper or true meaning of the entire earthly order. With Machiavelli, however, the understanding of politics shifted to comprehension of the reality of newly emerging western states in which power was viewed more and more as something in and of itself, without any necessary reference beyond itself. Moreover, political power was no longer viewed as a subordinate element to something universal; it could now stand alone in separate "states."[4]

With the emergence and growth of this new conception of politics as concentrated power, a vacuum also emerged and began to grow—a vacuum of political meaning, identity, and order as far as the "one world" was concerned. The process by which that vacuum has been filled is essentially the history of modern nationalism and internationalism since the time of Machiavelli. The modern state has emerged in the form of a new kind of power organization, and in order for it to find its proper place and purpose in the world, it has had to define for itself certain "goals" or "ends" to be achieved individually and separately. The modern state or political entity is no longer understood as part of a single divine ordering of this one world, but is now thought of as something in itself. And the way in which people are supposedly able to decide whether a particular state is legitimate and good is by means of an evaluation of the goals which that state is trying to reach by the use of its own limited power. First in the West, and now throughout the world, politics have become a matter of independent power units, each reaching for its own goals.

To illustrate, let us consider some of the goals that have been adopted by modern states to justify and/or to fulfill their existence as centers of organized power. What was the meaning of the organization of force in the new nation states of France and Spain four hundred years ago? These were two of the first great modern political powers. If we immerse ourselves in the study of that era, one of the things we can see, in contrast to the Holy Roman Empire, the Roman Empire, and the Chinese Middle Kingdom, is that the "goal" of newly won power was simply the glory and growth of Spain, the glory and growth of France. The meaning of power, in other words, had to do with the intention of the new governments to bring about a full and glorious preeminence for their own nations. Each one had its own culture and its own understanding of what would constitute its "glory."

Or take as another example, the goal of those who captured power in the American colonies during and after the revolutionary struggle with Britain. The goal was to achieve a non-monarchical, republican federation, defined by the "self-rule" of the people. To most colonists, it appeared to be entirely legitimate to use force to cut off British rule, to take control of "power" in order to try to build a different kind of political system.

A third example is France, at the time of the revolution of 1789. The goal of that revolutionary takeover of power was to change the social structure from its domination by hierarchical authorities, including the Church and the aristocracy, to a new populist egalitarianism. Here the "goal" of a democratic society was sufficient to justify the use of force which would put the control of power into new hands.

Another case in point is the revolution in Russia in 1917. The meaning of that takeover of power was hypothetically to put an end to all use of power or force. The revolution, as Lenin saw it, would become legitimate in the eyes of the world once the state itself disappeared, and when the very use of power would be abolished. Today, as the goal of a non-coercive communist society becomes an increasingly distant future hope in the Soviet Union, it is possible to see even more clearly how the goal has been separated from the organization of power which that goal is meant to justify. People living in the Soviet Union are supposed to be willing to wait as long as necessary for the new world to arrive, and in the meantime the power of the state which is controlled by the Communist Party can be used for whatever purposes the party deems necessary.

A final example brings us nearer home. The legitimacy

of governmental power in the United States and Canada today is sustained in large measure by the general popular consensus that these governments are doing their best to bring about increasing economic prosperity. North American governments control power in order to achieve the great society, the new frontier, the further advancement of science and technology.[5] Most Americans and Canadians accept the legitimacy of American or Canadian power in terms of the goals which have been announced, even if after many years they still do not see sufficient evidence that these goals are going to be reached. For instance, even if all the evidence suggests that the rich and poor in the United States are growing farther apart rather than closer together in income, most Americans continue to justify the existing governmental establishment in terms of the ultimate goal of prosperity for everyone.

Justice, Power, and World Order

The point of our argument thus far is not to suggest that ancient China, the Roman Empire, and the Holy Roman Empire were ideally *just* political orders and that what we now have is thoroughly *unjust*. The way in which power was used in those empires did not always, or even usually, lead to justice. Nor does the use of power today inevitably lead to injustice. The point is simply that the control of power today has been separated to such an extent from any normative conception of a just "world order" that it more or less lives a life of its own, tied only to certain future goals or ends which separate states are seeking to achieve for themselves individually. The state as a power entity, as an organization of force, is oriented toward certain goals that justify its control and use of that power. A universal norm of "justice" or the idea of a "just world order" is not an integral or ordinary part of our thinking about power and politics today. Justice as an international political norm is either ignored altogether, or is identified with one of the "goals" that a particular state has adopted.

Justice for the Marxist is identified with the communist world of the future. That means, of course, that there is no way for anyone to ask if the present use of power by the Communist Party in the Soviet Union or China is just or unjust from an international point of view. All one can do, if one accepts the communist view, is to live by faith, believing that one day the present use of force will justify itself. One is not allowed to bring a normative question into the context of contemporary Marxist-Leninist theory, as for example, the question of whether the "dictatorship of the proletariat" is good or bad for the world at the present time. That is an impossible question; there is no place for it in communist thought. The mindset of the Marxist is that the old capitalist order is illegitimate and ought to be destroyed, and that the new order toward which we are headed is good and must be built. But the Marxist has no way to get at the justice or injustice of the present socialist dictatorship in the context of the present international situation.

In the modern international order the task of government is thought to be fulfilled if separate governments do either or both of two things. First, a government may legitimately attempt merely to preserve its own power or to preserve the existence and power of the state in which it functions. Most of the support for huge defense budgets, the spending of billions of dollars on weapons, comes about because we assume that it is legitimate for a government simply to try to preserve its own power. Machiavelli would have argued that the first task of the government is to get power and hold it firmly. One of the reasons why it is very difficult for the rich world to begin thinking about a different international structure at an economic level is that our framework of assumptions begins with the priority of *our* state holding and enhancing what it has already got. It is antithetical to the entire framework of modern politics for a state to think that it can enhance its meaning, its stature, its justice, or its place in the world by giving up anything that it already possesses or by purposefully limiting itself.[6]

Another reason is that in most countries the mere preservation of power is not enough. Usually a certain percentage of the national budget is spent to push the country toward other goals. Most people in the United States, for example, want economic growth and better economic opportunities. They want better health care, better social and public services, and better education for their children. These goals, then, must be sought by the American government. Justice need not exist at this moment either within the domestic circumstances of the United States or in its relations with other countries; it is enough that the government is able to convince the voters that it is headed in the right direction—a direction that will eventually bring greater prosperity and greater justice to everyone in the world without anyone in the United States losing what he or she now possesses. The majority of American citizens can live with the present order if the promises for the future look bright and peaceful enough. It is difficult for the majority to understand why the poor and powerless of this world are not equally as patient and longsuffering.

But what this means for the international situation is that instead of having a framework for thinking about world justice, we simply have the confrontation of "powers," of states with states. That kind of international "order" is the fruit of the competing efforts of various states, each attempting to make its own way in the world. Thus the agreements that states come up with from time to time, establishing rules for the conduct of mutual trade, the procedure of beginning and ending wars, or the kind of mutual defense organizations they should construct—those agreements are made in *ad hoc* fashion, one day at a time, accidentally here, with a little planning there, while each country keeps seeking its own interests. Until the twentieth century this international arrangement was relatively stable because most people lived *within* the borders of their separate states. Moreover, only a small amount of power was controlled by each state. No airplanes and no nuclear weapons existed that could be flown or thrown around the world. The total world population was relatively small, with people in one part of the world (China, for example) largely unaware of what was happening in another part of the world (say, Europe). In the nineteenth century, in other words, there was still room in the world for a variety of independent billiard balls to roll around and hit each other only occasionally without creating too much chaos.

But today we are reaching the end of the relatively free independence of nations. The lives of almost all people in the world no longer revolve simply around the decisions and institutions and relationships that exist *within* their own countries. Highly interdependent Canadian and American relations exemplify the growing interconnectedness among all countries. The interconnections among Western countries, and now also among the countries of the rich world and the poor world, are becoming so complex that the very idea of international relations based primarily on the sovereign independence of states, is no longer adequate to deal with the real world. It is no longer possible to imagine that a world order can be built solely upon the unilateral decisions and bilateral relationships of separate states.[7] The world economy is no longer organized merely on the basis of the decisions that the United States (or any other country) makes independently with another country about trade.

Power vs Justice

Precisely at this point we face the growing confrontation between "power" and "justice" in the world. Competing powers are increasingly creating a world that contradicts and makes impossible the exercise of justice. What we have in the world is, on the one hand, the growing awareness of the limits of the power struggle when it comes to meeting human needs. What is taking place in many United Nations conferences, in the North-South economic dialogue, and in many other international meetings, is the result of a growing desire of many nations and leaders to find cooperative, international ways to face common problems. It is becoming increasingly clear to many people that nations must begin to establish international structural conditions and institutions that will last—structures and institutions that will help to determine the future decisions of countries.

But on the other hand, we still have the continuing, even growing arms race, which is an integral part of the older international setting of many separate states, each one going its own way on the basis of its own power. The new states that have entered the world community since World War II, as independent entities, learned from the modern West that the use of self-interested power frequently gives a nation more influence than cooperation in the short run. Even to this day the states that gain the most themselves are those that exert the most power. The American economy continues to grow; it continues to take a large share of world economic potential, and it frequently obtains a good deal for itself. Since World War II the United States has seldom found itself in a predicament where its dominant position in the world has been threatened. Therefore, what Third World countries have learned is that for all their talk about international cooperation or about how the United States or the United Nations should aid their cause, little happens if they themselves do not exert power. Oil-producing countries have realized that they can only get their own way by using power and the threat of power—in this case by withholding oil supplies. Many states are spending millions of dollars for military weapons while their people lack the necessities of life.

Today we live with two different outlooks on the world, politically speaking. On the one hand, we believe that international cooperation is a good and necessary thing; we believe that nations ought to cooperate rather than fight and threaten each other. Canada and the United States would probably never think of going to war with each other;

problems, we believe, can be worked out. On the other hand, we continue to think that each nation ought to look after itself first; that it ought to build up its own power and force so that it can manipulate other countries in order to get its own way.

We have an ideological struggle in the world. We see a continuing development of the historical pattern of the past five hundred years which cannot be dismissed overnight; a tradition that functions on the principle that international relations among nations will be built solely or primarily on the basis of actions by independent, self-interested, sovereign powers. But we are also now beginning to realize that unless there is a cooperative arrangement and agreement from the start on the conditions and rules of global interdependence, we are all lost. In other words, we live today with an increasingly clear pattern of confrontation between "power" and "justice"—between two different ideas about how the world should be politically structured. Thus, while cynical despair builds up among those who believe that the bomb will certainly be dropped before international peace is achieved, at the same time a sense of hope continues among those who believe that international cooperation can be institutionalized, as a result of the growing awareness of people that we all live in *one* world.

The Opportunity for Christian Service

At this point in history, Christians have the greatest opportunity to be of political service. In the debates and discussions about power and justice in the world today, Christians should be raising and clarifying some of the most basic questions about politics and world order. What is the task of the state? What is the appropriate place and task of international institutions? What ought to be the structure and limits of international institutions and agreements? Should there be more multilateral institutions and treaties? What is the proper role of the United Nations? What kind of new political structures with a transnational character ought to be built, and why? In order to be able to ask these questions with wisdom and understanding, North American Christians need to hear what people in Africa, Latin America and Asia have to say about the justice and injustice of their present situations. We cannot understand what form international justice should take until we can begin, as Christians across all of the world's borders, to discuss these questions together. And this is a different matter than Americans asking what the United States can do *for* the world, because even if we have the best of intentions, the unilateral act of one country toward another country is still a different kind of decision, a different kind of act than that of two or more countries working together from the start, establishing some political program or policy.

What can Canadian, American, Mexican, European, and Chinese Christians, working together, say about the relationships that ought to exist among Canada, the United States, Mexico, Europe, and China? *That* is the question!

From this standpoint it is amazing that a "Christian International" does not exist in the world. There is a Communist International, even with its ups and downs, its weaknesses and its strengths. Right now its unity is fractured by its many competing centers of power. But a unified vision of Communist International has long existed because it has as its ultimate goal the fundamental doctrine of communism—the communist order that transcends the limits of the state and the interstate system. Yet, if there has ever been a confession made in history that the true meaning of justice and human community transcends the limits of particular states, it is the confession inaugurated in the person and work of Christ. The Christian vision of the world, which has its roots in the prophetic anticipations of Amos and Isaiah, is a vision of the coming King who will be the King of all kings, a King who will call His people to a global communion and fellowship for the service of all mankind, and for the sake of justice and peace worldwide.

Christians have not pursued that vision properly or sufficiently. They have acted as though it is not even necessary, since the Gospel concerns only spiritual life and not politics, and politically they have become satisfied simply to be Americans or Canadians or some other nationality.

But the Bible will not allow us to live with such an outlook. The biblical vision is a vision of a kingdom that transcends American, Canadian and European interests. One of the most prominent evidences of Christian weakness in the world today is the failure to pursue this political vision together in international community for the sake of justice for all people. A distinctive Christian contribution to international peace and justice cannot be developed without Christians throughout the world coming together to share their insights, their abilities, and their God-given gifts. In the face of growing conflict between "the powers" and the need for global "justice," Christians should be coming together on the basis of their allegiance to the only true King, in order to shed some light on the character of justice that should prevail in the present world.[8]

2

America First?

America's Rise to Power

Stephan E. Ambrose begins his book on America's *Rise to Globalism* with the following remarkable description of the position of the United States in the world in 1939:

As Franklin Roosevelt began his sixth year as President, the United States had an army of 185,000 officers and men with an annual budget of less than $500 million. America had no military alliances and no American troops were stationed in any foreign country. Except on the high seas and within North America, the nation had no offensive capability at all. The overwhelming sentiment within the country was isolationist. Most Americans felt that their country had been cheated by the European powers at the Versailles Conference at the conclusion of World War I and they were determined that never again would the United States be dragged into European disputes. America was willing, even anxious, to trade with foreign powers, but that was all. The single most important fact about American foreign policy in early 1939 was that the great bulk of the American people felt little obligation to become involved in foreign wars, much less that their nation should establish a hegemony over Western Europe or Southeast Asia. American security, the *sine qua non* of foreign policy, seemed assured, not because of American alliances or military might but because of the distance between America and any potential enemy.[1]

At the start of the 1980s we are well aware that an almost unbelievable change has taken place. The American defense budget is now over $150 billion; American troops are stationed all over the globe; for more than thirty years the United States has been the number one power in the world, and after a decade of uncertainty following the trauma of Vietnam, the United States is once again planning to increase its defense spending by billions of dollars each year in order to try to remain on top.

But the question we want to ask is, "Should the purpose of American foreign policy be to keep America number one and to seek American interests first?" Our question is not primarily an historical one about how the United States got into its present position. Nor is it a question about foreign policy strategies in a world where the Soviet Union is a military equal to the United States, where energy resources are scarce, and where economic demands from other countries are growing in intensity. Rather, the question concerns the norm or principle that should ideally rule and guide foreign policy. The United States *is* the world's dominant power; but should it direct its policies toward the goal of serving its own interest first and trying to remain in that position?

The interpretations of how and why the United States has become so powerful are numerous. Some emphasize the expanding economic interests that motivated American leaders, particularly following the great depression. Others stress the almost accidental character of America's rise to power following World War II, when the country filled much of the power vacuum left by the devastation of Europe and the collapse of British, French, and other European empires around the world. Still others are impressed with the radical change brought about within the military bureaucracy and the executive branch of the federal government by the

development and use of nuclear weapons.[2] All of these interpretations along with other factors must be taken into account in any effort to understand the historical context in
which we are asking our questions about American foreign
policy goals and procedures.

Six Important Characteristics
of the Contemporary World

Let us briefly consider the contemporary international
context, because the past forty or fifty years have witnessed
more than America's rise to global power; very little else has
remained unchanged. American power is related to a swiftly
changing world. Six features seem to stand out as primary
determinants at present.

Nuclear Power. Clearly the states of the world, especially the
United States and the Soviet Union, have not yet learned how
to live with *nuclear weapons* that were developed during
World War II and which are still being multiplied, refined,
and "improved." American pride in its new atomic power
was a key factor in determining its foreign policy during the
1950s and early 1960s. However, the development of nuclear
weapons by the Soviet Union and other nations, and the
multiplying international tensions and turmoils which nuclear
weapons can do nothing to solve, have made it increasingly
clear that a successful foreign policy requires more than a
gigantic nuclear capability. Yet, after years of cold war, guerrilla war, interventionist war, limited war, protectionist war,
and liberationist war, the nuclear question remains unsolved.
The very limited success and the exceedingly long period of
negotiations toward Strategic Arms Limitation Treaties
(SALT) bear testimony to the unresolved difficulties inherent
in a state's possession of the "ultimate" weapon.[3]

Bipolar Confrontation. After World War II, two tremendous
power vacuums were created by the defeat of Germany and

Japan. The United States and the Soviet Union rushed to fill those vacuums by means of direct intervention as well as through the development of security alliances. For more than fifteen years the world saw the growth of new regional organizations such as NATO and the Warsaw Pact. The result was a world divided basically in two—a *bipolar world* divided *militarily* between East and West in a cold war confrontation. Richard J. Barnet argues that as a result of the post-war military and ideological competition between the United States and the Soviet Union a profound change took place in American society. Beginning with the mobilization in World War II, he explains, "the United States organized for war. The essentials of those organizational changes remain to this day."[4] Thus the United States became permanently organized for war.

A sharply divided bipolar world has gradually taken on some of the features of *multipolarity*, but sharp divisions and massive military preparedness remain.

Technological Maturity. Another major factor in the contemporary world has been the coming to maturity of one of this century's dominant religions, namely, *technologism.* According to Canadian philosopher, George Grant, American actions in Vietnam might be viewed by some as simple "ruthlessness and banal callousness," but that is an inadequate interpretation.

> It must be remembered that the exigencies of imperialism have to be justified to the public (particularly to the second order managers) under the banner of freedom and a liberating modernization . . . North America stands for the future of hope, a people of good will bringing the liberation of progress to the world.[5]

But what constitutes the means for achieving progress and freedom? The means is technology, and the drive to use technology is so strong, Grant points out, because "it is carried on by men who still identify what they are doing with the liberation of mankind."[6]

Nowhere has the technological drive been more powerful than in America, and nowhere more significant in America than in the development of foreign policy. Barnet says that the "tyranny of technique pervades the whole national security bureaucracy,"[7] and he cites W.W. Rostow (a top presidential assistant in the Johnson administration for three years) as the technocrat who "put together the most coherent philosophical statement about the use of American power."

> Rostow had the optimism and the naïveté and the nerve to visualize the denouement of the American Century. It was to be the technocrat's peace. Vietnam was Armageddon. The communist scavenger would slink back into the night, defeated, and the American elect would proceed to organize the peace through technology. The poor would be helped to achieve the "take-off" to a "high mass consumption" economy within a system of stability and order. Rostow sees "a new day in which organized violence finally ends." It will come through the spread of American technology and technique throughout the world, for according to the impervious Rostovian faith, "aggressive impulses diminish in technologically mature societies."[8]

Multipolarity. One of the changes most difficult for Westerners to understand has been the emergence of the *Third World*. The Third World is made up of the people and states that have refused to identify completely with either side of the East-West bipolarity. The Third World is the non-industrialized, underdeveloped, mostly dark-skinned world— often poverty-stricken. It is the world which even today is economically exploited, insufficiently aided, sometimes protected, and usually misunderstood by the wealthy and powerful nations of the world. The Third World is most of Africa, Asia, Latin America, and Indonesia. American foreign policy, directed by a simplistic technocratic faith in progress flowing forth from the United States, has not yet produced much of lasting significance in relation to the Third World.[9]

Business Expansionism and Foreign Policy. Yet another development since World War II has been the increasing influence of American business and industry on the structure of the country's foreign policy. Foreign policy is often guided by the goal of supporting and encouraging the growth of American enterprises at home and abroad without sufficient consideration of other interests or even of the government's main responsibility, that of seeking justice both domestically and internationally. The Marshall Plan, which helped to rebuild Europe after the war, is often noted for its success in aiding Europe while at the same time advancing American industry. But when we look at American policy in relation to both the rich and the poor nations of the world, we can see failures as well as successes. One of the "guiding stars" of American foreign policy since 1945, according to Ambrose, has been to open up doors for American enterprise.

> The enormous expansion in American production and financial predominance became the central factor in world economics. American corporate investment abroad increased astronomically and the government assumed the obligation of protecting—indeed, encouraging—those investments. But one of the tragedies of American foreign policy was that the United States reached the imperialistic stage at a time when the peoples of the exploited nations were increasingly determined that they would no longer be ruled by others, expecially white men.[10]

Richard Barnet describes the impact of "business expansionism" in poor countries this way:

> The drive of the developed countries, particularly the United States to increase the flow of consumer products to what is really the undeveloping world through branch plants and subsidized trade creates demands and diffuses tastes that are new to traditional societies. The notion that consumption is the key to happiness is a basic cultural value of developed societies. Consumerism is creating social and psychological

problems in the United States, but its effects in poor countries are disastrous. Aggressive advertising and marketing in the undeveloping countries have created demands that cannot be satisfied. The "revolution of rising expectations" is a cruel hoax, for the products poor people are taught to want and hope for are usually beyond their reach and in most cases are exactly what they do not need. In a country without public transportation the marketing of a few cars is destructive. The need is basic transportation for all, not speed or comfort for a few. Tobacco, Coca-Cola, and other destructive or nutritionally useless products are being effectively marketed to poor people in the undeveloping world who subsist on less than fifteen hundred calories a day.[11]

Pragmatic Approach. Pragmatism is another of the chief factors shaping foreign policy today. Bob Goudzwaard says that pragmatism, as a philosophy of life, is one of the most potent movements of our time. "The question whether a certain action is morally or ethically correct is asked less and less," he explains, "and more and more people are only interested in what the practical effect of an action will be. If there is a desired effect, then an action causing it is declared to have been the correct action."[12] Barnet recognizes that the pragmatic approach to foreign policy has sometimes permitted men with little understanding of world affairs or of government principles to give leadership in the formation of U.S. policy.

> Many of the national security managers prided themselves on taking a systems analysis approach to foreign relations— collect the facts, calculate the costs and benefits, outline the possible options, and select the best course. The problem was that they did not know enough that was relevant about the rest of the world to understand what system they were operating in. They saw no need to understand foreign societies they thought they knew how to manage.[13]

Can the "America First" Strategy Guide U.S. Foreign Policy?

In the global context we have just described, what should guide American foreign policy? Can the American government simply aim to keep the country number one? Should the government seek American interests first? With these questions in mind, let us look at the six characteristics we have mentioned.

First. Are nuclear weapons something that the United States can control and use in a way that enhances its own interests first without enhancing or harming the interests of others at the same time? Can the United States simply aim for its own preeminence in this regard? Of course not, and all American efforts to establish multilateral treaties limiting or banning nuclear weapons demonstrate its awareness that its own interests are tied up with the common interests of all states. The real question is this: "How will the United States work together with other countries so that all of them can control nuclear weapons for the sake of peace?" If American nuclear power remains number one (which is not necessarily good or bad), that will be a side effect or consequence that ought *not* to be sought for its own sake.

Second. Can the United States seek its own interests first or maintain its status in either a *bipolar* or a *multipolar* world by remaining permanently organized for war, even if most of the wars that it might enter will reduce its power and wealth? No, of course not! The Korean conflict did not diminish Chinese or Russian power and enhance American power, but only aided the military growth of both communist giants. Vietnam did not prove that America was preeminent, but showed how a certain kind of guerrilla warfare can outlast and wear down even the most powerful military machine. Massive military preparedness, even when necessary, cannot assure a country that its own interests will be served or that its status will be maintained. Other goals and purposes must be sought by civilian and military leaders.

Third. Can technological growth guarantee the United States its lead position? Certainly not! Swiss watchmakers, Japanese car manufacturers, and Russian missile engineers have found ways to advance beyond American capabilities regardless of how much money or effort the United States puts into technology. Technology is not something that one country can monopolize even if it strives to do so. Moreover, an unlimited faith and excessive investment in technology can sap energy from other human activities that are essential if people and states are to be strong. Hitler's Germany was technologically advanced, but we hardly admire the character of that regime. What kinds of human goals are we encouraging in the United States with so much emphasis placed upon technological growth? Do we really want to be number one in tank production or assembly-line speed, if it means being number six in health care, or number ten in having a morally trustworthy government, or number twenty in urban safety? When we talk about America being "Number One," what do we mean? Number one in what sense? What priorities will determine American interests?

Fourth. Should we be thankful for Third World poverty and instability because it highlights American strength? Or could it be that real strength, even for the United States, lies in a more just world order where other countries become more self-sufficient, more productive, and more mature participants in defining the global context in which all states function? Perhaps the biblical admonition has something to say to states as well as to individuals: "For whosoever will save his life shall lose it: and whosoever will lose his life for my sake shall find it" (Matthew 16:25).

Fifth. Will the continuing advancement of American business interests around the world keep the United States in

35

its number one position? Are those the interests that the American government should watch over above all others? Once again, the answer is no! The United States is more than a giant business community. What it can contribute to the global community is more than economic expertise. Moreover, inflation, unemployment, recession, and balance of trade deficits in the United States cannot be avoided by the country working independently. These are global problems. International cooperation is required at the start, not simply at the end of the line. But cooperation requires that states seek their common interests together. Other states will not be roped into serving American interests before their own any more than the United States is going to serve other states' interests first.

Sixth. Finally, we must ask whether hardnosed pragmatism is the one sure method for guaranteeing America's privileged place in the world. No. The problem with pragmatism is that it leaves unexamined the starting assumptions. All that pragmatism can do is to try to solve problems within the framework of assumptions that have already been accepted. But this means that any faith in pragmatism is a faith in yesterday's assumptions; it means putting our future in the hands of yesterday's visionaries. Has it not become clear, however, that the United States needs some new understanding, some new purposes, some new goals in a world that bears no resemblance to pre-industrialized Europe, or to pre-World War II Asia, or to pre-energy crisis North America? A number one America in 1950 will not necessarily be number one in 1990. The question that the United States must ask, but which the pragmatists cannot answer, is "What *ought* to guide U.S. policymaking now?"

We see, then, that the goal of "America First" or of "Keeping the United States Number One" cannot function as a meaningful goal of foreign policy. It is a romantic wish for happiness and security that substitutes for genuine political norms and purposes. If exclusive American interests are served, and if the United States remains a strong country in the world, it will be as a result of the countless decisions that many states make with or without American concurrence. America's role in the world will depend on the degree to which it can cooperate with other states in defining a common world order. Its strength will rise or fall as a consequence of the goals that it seeks. Its strength will depend upon the norms that it obeys and upon the justice or injustice that it promotes. Being number one is not a status that a state can obtain or maintain by simple act of will.

3

Christian Principle and Political Reality

Realism vs Idealism

It is one thing to recognize that a wide range of global limits places restrictions on the unbridled exercise of sovereignty by a country such as the United States. It is quite another thing, however, to argue that the United States *ought* to promote international justice and not simply its own interests. What is the basis for a moral argument of this kind? Is it proper? Isn't it too idealistic to imagine that global justice will ever be achieved? If the United States tries to act justly but other countries act unjustly, won't it be the primary loser? Wouldn't it be far more realistic for the United States to act in a way that serves its own interests since it is probably safe to assume that other countries will primarily be looking after their own interests?

Many scholars and critics of foreign policy have argued that the United States acted far too idealistically in the late nineteenth and early twentieth centuries. President Woodrow Wilson was one of the worst offenders. He promoted the establishment of the League of Nations with the hope that eventually most countries of the world would become democratic, peace loving, and obedient to international law. But such idealism proved to be a faulty guide for foreign policymaking in a world where states seldom pursue a high moral purpose. Today the ruling principle in making foreign policy, both in the United States and elsewhere, is *realism*—a term that suggests hardnosed, self-interested action by officials on behalf of their own country.

Should we accept the principle of realism? Are there only two options: realism or idealism? Is there any room for principled, Christian responsibility in foreign policymaking? If we ask these questions or others such as, "What direction ought American policy to take in order for justice to be done to other nations and peoples?" or, "What kind of legitimate world order ought Christians to be helping to build?" or, "What principles ought to guide Christians in their decisions to support or to reject the foreign policies of their own governments?" If we ask these questions, we must be prepared to face the criticism of the realists who argue that the world order we would *ideally* wish to build might not have the possibility of actual *realization*. We must be prepared to answer the charge that idealistic discussions of moral principle might have some meaning in theological debate but are irrelevant in making *real* foreign policy decisions.

In its simplest form the problem has been posed by the title of one of Reinhold Niebuhr's early books, *Moral Man and Immoral Society*. Niebuhr argues that while it is quite legitimate and even realistic to discuss the moral responsibilities of individuals, it is quite another matter to discuss the responsibilities of social institutions and especially of states in an international context that is almost lawless. States can hardly ever act morally. We can talk of international politics as *amoral*, at best, and at worst, as *immoral*.[1]

Before adopting too quickly a defensive posture in face of this so-called realism in order to plead for the right to inject morality into the discussion, let us consider what it is that we are being asked to accept with this framework of realism versus idealism; immorality versus morality.

At first the realist argument comes across as sufficiently sound and plausible to win our uncritical acceptance. Morality, it is argued, is a personal thing that has meaning only if individuals can be held accountable for their acts. Within ordinary societies there are countless human communities and religious systems from the family to the courts, from the schools to the churches, that accomplish precisely this function of holding individuals accountable. But states are not individuals, and insufficient numbers and kinds of supranational institutions exist to hold them accountable to and for one another in relation to some universal, supranational, moral principle. If a single state were to act unilaterally on the basis of a moral code that is applicable to individuals, it would very likely run into the greater evil of endangering its own existence, and thus the very lives of its citizens. Consequently, states must act as states, not as individual persons, and the result might appear to be quite immoral from the vantage point of the moral individual.

There is more, however, to the realist's argument. Having established what appears to be the impossibility of morally guided action by states in the international arena, the realist tries to justify a state's seemingly immoral actions on the grounds that states have no choice but to seek their own survival and self-interest. Whether one believes that a state's self-interest acts are the result of human sinfulness or whether one simply recognizes the fact that states have always acted in self-protective, self-enhancing ways, it remains the case, so the realist argues, that this is the *reality* of the international arena and that states do not have the freedom to act as if this were not so.

But look again at that argument. How have we described the state? What have we assumed about how states are forced to act? We have used the word "self" several times in connection with the idea of "national self-interest." And the word "act," clearly conveying the impression that states act as integral entities, making certain policies that express the state's "will." But what is the meaning of these terms? Isn't the realist arguing that states cannot be treated as moral persons? How then can we be expected to think of states as immoral, or self-centered persons? If states are not "selves" capable of *moral* acts and responsibilities, then why should we grant that they are "selves" capable of *immoral* acts?

What has happened here is that the realists have rejected a framework of moral meaning for states on the grounds that the state is not a moral agent, but at the same time, they have retained a framework of personal, behavioral meaning, however analogically or metaphorically, in order to explain and interpret a state's actions in the international context. In that context, a state's "self-interested actions" are then justified as necessary and legitimate. The result is a very subtle swindle or self-deception. While our attention was focused on the question of morality, we were led to believe that states could not be expected to act according to moral principle. But if we turn our attention away from this inadequately framed moral question and focus instead on the meaning of "person" and "self," of "will" and "act," then we will see that the question of morality is not really at issue; the more fundamental question is about two different kinds of "persons" that can "act," and about two different sorts of principles that *ought* to guide them, given their respectively different identities.

Upon closer examination in fact, we find that Reinhold Niebuhr and others, when discussing international relations, have not relinquished issues of morality and normativity at all. They have continued to argue quite normatively about how states *ought* to act in order to preserve themselves and the world order. Realism is not opposed to all principles; it does not argue against every kind of norm; it has merely tried to free itself from a kind of moralism that it finds unacceptable, and has attempted to establish a different framework of principles for international politics that can justify self-interested acts by states.

The Principle of Justice vs Realism/Idealism

It would seem then, that we must reject the problem in the way that the realists have posed it for us. They have not unveiled political *reality* in a way that proves that "morality" is uncertain, questionable, and out of bounds. Instead, their argument has only helped to show that the *entire reality*, the *full reality*, of international politics must be called into question, including the very identity of states and the principles by which states ought to act. Posing the problem this way might lead us to reject idealism, but it should also lead us to reject a great deal of what passes for *realism* which is, in fact, a dogmatic argument for a particular kind of "best possible" world—an argument that we should find unacceptable if we are truly concerned with international justice.

It should also be noted here that much of contemporary realism, identified with the ideas of Hans Morgenthau, George F. Kennan, and others, is deeply indebted to many Christians from Reinhold Niebuhr to St. Augustine. At the same time, idealism, identified with the ideas of Woodrow Wilson, John Hobson, and others, is equally indebted to a long Christian tradition.[2] It is not only the pagan humanists, therefore, who have maliciously swindled the Christians in this case. To the contrary, serious ambiguities and inadequacies in the Christian conceptions of political order, from Augustine to the present, are partially responsible for the failure of modern Christians to transcend the framework of the idealist/realist debate.

If we try to approach the problems of international politics in a new way, it will probably be relatively easy for most of us to turn away from the moral idealism that realists have been criticizing for years, precisely because idealism does not deal very directly or completely with reality. However, if we reject idealism, we should do so not as the realists do, but by way of our own self-criticism which can demonstrate that Christian morality has nothing to do with wishful idealism.

Biblical tradition does not present morality as an abstract ideal, but as a covenantal framework of concrete norms for many different *real* institutions—from marriage and the family to churches and kingdoms. No biblical grounds exist for treating kings and generals and judges as though their responsibilities could be defined by some ideal political system or as though their individual responsibilities could be defined apart from their political offices in real states. Nor did God's Word come to those generals, kings and judges as if they were priests or fathers or deacons. Those of us who stand in the biblical tradition should be quick to reject a "moral idealism" which, by its very abstract and truncated character, proves to be inapplicable to nations and states as they really function in this world.

If, then, we refuse to be deterred from our efforts to clarify norms for national foreign policies and international justice, it is not because we are pious idealists ever hopeful that one day people and states might become "good," but rather because we know that the reality of evil which manifests itself in every human institution and relationship can never finally escape the wrath and judgment of God who holds on to this *one real* world by His authoritative and gracious Word, and who calls people and nations to heed His demands for justice and mercy and faithful stewardship. A biblically grounded, normative framework that has meaning for international politics today will not be a vague pious ideal, a mere hope for a better world, an irrelevant legal or moral fiction that cannot work because it does not ever come to grips with the realities of political power.

If we, however, find it possible to turn away from moral idealism with relative ease, it might be more difficult for us to take our distance from political realism. It might be helpful if, at this juncture, we deal directly with a figure who represents, to a significant degree, a realistic outlook and approach.

Henry Kissinger

Henry Kissinger is a complex figure, not easily reduced to a simple classification; nevertheless, it is not improper to view him as a creative realist. He has certainly approached his responsibilities as theorist and statesman with the assumption that the reality of international politics consists of competing powers which are not free to act on the basis of irrelevant ideals. Moreover, Kissinger is the student par excellence of nineteenth-century Europe's balance of power arrangement and the statesman who made a great effort to try to bring the United States to see the contemporary world for what it *really* is today—a multipolar, global field of competing powers that must achieve some kind of stable balance if global peace is to be preserved.

It is interesting to note, therefore, that in his earliest book, *A World Restored* (1964),[3] Kissinger made a very strong case for the fact that political power is not all that constitutes international politics. Statesmen cannot be satisfied with the mere "balance of power," argues Kissinger; they must attempt to build a "particular," "historical" equilibrium that all of the states can accept as legitimate for the process of their ongoing interactions and adjustments. The problem faced at the Congress of Vienna in 1815, he says,

> . . . was to create an order in which change should be brought about through a sense of obligation, instead of through an assertion of power. For the difference between a revolutionary order and a *healthy* legitimate one is not the possibility of change, but the mode of its accomplishment. A "legitimate" order, as long as it is not stagnant, achieves its transformations through acceptance, and this presupposes a consensus on the nature of a just arrangement.[4]

In another passage Kissinger made the argument universal and states it even more strongly:

> The stability of any international system depends on at least two factors: the degree to which its components feel secure

and the extent to which they agree on the "justice" or "fairness" of existing arrangements . . . Considerations of power are not enough, however, since they turn every disagreement into a test of strength. Equilibrium is needed for stability: moral consensus is essential for spontaneity. In the absence of agreement as to what constitutes a "just" or "reasonable" claim, no basis for negotiation exists.[5]

It would be a mistake, then, for us to imagine that nineteenth-century Europe was stable merely because military forces were balanced, or to believe that the international situation in Europe during that period can be described accurately by reference merely to its shifts of power alliances and the relative absence of war. Unless one notices the moral legitimacy of the order, that is, the acceptance of the order as essentially just by most of the states, then one misses an essential part of the *reality*. What the statesmen of that day struggled with, and what the political scientists and historians of our day must take into account, is the full scope of that international situation which included the decisions made concerning the nature of a mutually acceptable order.

This insight alone should be enough to give us some clues to the perspective of the realist today. It is one thing to argue, as realists do, that independent states in a world of anarchy cannot afford to ignore the reality of that anarchy. Agreed! It is quite another thing, however, to argue, as some realists also do, that the goal of achieving a power balance, in order to maximize national interests, is the correct principle that *ought* always to guide the statesman in his efforts to deal with other states.

By describing the character of nineteenth-century Europe's moral settlement, one may not thereby arrive at the *normative* conclusion that the nineteenth century's particular solution was what *ought* to have been established at that time. Nor may one arrive at the conclusion that such a solution reveals the true norm which *ought* to continue to guide states today. On the basis of historical evidence, the only legitimate conclusions at which one can arrive are:

● that there is an international situation that does impose itself on individual states in a way that does not leave them free unilaterally to ignore or change it; and

● that in attempting to deal with one another in an anarchic situation, states do make decisions that contribute either to a legitimate and healthy order or to an illegitimate and revolutionary arrangement.

Consequently, the moral or normative questions always remain open at every stage of political decision-making in every historical situation.

As we noticed earlier, a realistic approach to international politics cannot in fact be amoral; to the contrary, whether or not realists attempt to hide their normative judgments, their approach is one that leads to judgments about what *ought* to guide states in their foreign policy-making. The question that we must ask of Henry Kissinger, therefore, is what grounds does he have for arguing that a given arrangement or approach is the correct one?

In a recent study that examines Kissinger's major writings, up to 1975, James and Diane Dornan explain that Kissinger's position regarding the proper place of morality in foreign policy was clearly evident from the outset: "He rejected sole reliance upon the balance of power for purely pragmatic reasons, because it was inadequate to achieve stability, not because a 'legitimate' system was morally preferable."[6] Kissinger, in other words, is a moral relativist, interested only in the mutual acceptance by states of whatever international order can be established with relative stability.

The great task that belongs to the statesman, in Kissinger's view, is not that of trying to maximize an international order of justice, but of creatively manipulating a given situation in a way that allows states to go beyond it in the direction of greater stability. Kissinger has argued that the meaning of human life is found in the creative expression of personality; ". . . nothing can relieve man from his ultimate responsibility, from giving his own meaning to life, from

47

elevating himself above necessity . . ."[7] For the statesman this means nothing less than acting on the basis of a creative "intuition," following "his vision of the future," in order to avoid the danger of becoming a prisoner of events.[8]

But how does one gain the correct intuition? What grounds are there for believing that a particular "vision of the future" is the correct one? Kissinger's answer is that the autonomous creativity of the lonely statesman is the primary source of such a guide and norm. "Unfortunately," says Kissinger,

> "a call to greatness is often not understood by contemporaries," and "statesmen often share the fate of prophets, that they are without honor in their own country," because "their greatness is usually apparent only in retrospect when their intuition has become experience." Statesmen must have the courage of their convictions—they must "act as if their intuition were truth," attempting to "educate" their countrymen in the process.[9]

Surely if Henry Kissinger can appeal to the autonomous, creative intuition of the statesmen for the guiding norms that should shape the actions of nations, then we have every right to appeal to a historically-rooted, publicly-debated, Christian norm of global justice as a guide for the shaping of foreign policies. The debate that Christians should now be forcing, without any defensive hesitancy whatever, is the debate over the correct norms and principles and visions of the future which alone can lead to international justice, and to the means by which states can cooperate to achieve the demands of global justice. We should spend no more time derailed by the false dilemma of realism versus idealism.

Going Beyond Legal Formalities

If it is possible for Christians to get beyond a naïve idealism that merely hopes for a more rational, legal, peaceful world, and beyond a power-fixated realism that approaches international politics with a primary concern for enlarging and sustaining the national interest, then the most difficult next step for most of us may be that of gaining a sufficiently expanded view of public justice to enable us to get beyond the narrow confines of legal formalities. By "legal formalities" is meant those basic principles of Western liberal democracy that have relatively little to do with the actual identity and substantive tasks of the state, both domestically and internationally. The "legal formalities" are those negative limitations and procedural rules that tend to take the place of substantive political identity in the West.

Consider three of these formalities. The first is the doctrine of "human rights" those primarily individual freedoms upon which, it is believed, governments ought not to infringe or violate. The second is the doctrine of "popular sovereignty" which requires that some kind of formal, democratic, representative procedure be established for allowing citizens to exercise some control over the government that rules them. Third is the doctrine of *pacta sunt servanda*, which means that contracts or treaties, once agreed to, ought to be kept.

To argue that we need to get beyond the confines of these legal formalities does not mean that we should reject them. To the contrary, we should support those international efforts that will enhance the security of individuals in face of arbitrary governments—governments that do not respect basic human rights. We should support those efforts that will aid the growth of responsible, representative government. And we should continue to support the important principle of political trustworthiness that will encourage nations to abide by their treaty commitments.

But we delude ourselves if we think that these formal principles alone are sufficient to define the normative framework of national and international justice. We are mistaken if we believe that these constitute the primary moral goals of foreign policy. The internal substance of public justice does not come to light simply through following certain protective rules and procedures. Public justice in the twentieth century can become manifest only where there is an equitable and healthy development among many interwoven communities, both public and private. Justice within states and among them exists when all people enjoy adequate health care and education; when the proper balance is achieved among industries and agriculture, among educational programs and professional services, between social mobility and social stability, between rural and urban living centers; when a government can aid the growth of public harmony domestically in a way that does not require it to act unjustly against other nations and governments.

International Economic Order

Let us take just one contemporary example to illustrate this point. It has become especially clear since 1973 that the international economic arrangements established at the end of World War II with the International Monetary Fund, the General Agreement on Tariffs and Trade, and a few other charters and institutions, are inadequate to handle the international economic problems of today.[10] The chief principle of the post-war economic order was the doctrine of free trade which, it was assumed, was the best guide to economic efficiency and prosperity. But free trade leads to increasing international integration of domestic markets, which in turn advances international economic interdependence. Thus, by the time the United States was withdrawing from the Vietnam War, and by the time energy shortages and other problems began to surface, most of the free trading partners were experiencing serious economic and social disequilibria that could not be alleviated without government actions that were in violation of the free trade doctrine. The governments of these countries began to throw up protective tariff barriers and other "temporary safeguards" against free trade in order to alleviate balance of payments deficits, unemployment in certain sectors of their economies, and so forth.

According to British economist John Pinder,

> The disruption of weaker sectors and economies, the insta-
> bility of commodity and money markets, and the trans-
> mission of inflation or deflation from one open economy to
> another are now so pervasive that the exception [to the free
> trade principle] has become the rule: unless governments
> provide strong economic management, structural as well as
> conjunctural, and externally as well as domestically, free
> competition fails to maximize welfare, largely because of the
> oligopolistic strength of many firms and trade unions and
> because of the immobility of many factors of produc-
> tion . . .[11]

From Pinder's point of view, economically interdependent states have only two options. They can either retreat to a
full insulation of their economies from one another, or they
can adopt common policies to deal with common problems.
"In other words, the integration of markets needs either to be
replaced by a separation of markets or to be complemented
by an integration of policies"[12] Pinder urges that an integration of policies ought to be promoted because he believes that
the need for economic management by governments will continue to grow and that "technological and social forces are
pushing the modern economies toward greater interdependence, so that the economic and social costs of market
separation will [only] increase."[13]

Of course, we also know that the governments of North
America, Western Europe and Japan are no longer free to
deal *only* with one another. They are not alone in their growing interdependence. The Third World and even some of the
communist countries are also involved in this growing interdependence. The governments of almost all countries are
being driven to a serious reconsideration and probably to a
recreation of almost the entire international economic
system. The decisions that will be made in the years ahead
with regard to these issues may be more complex and will cer-

tainly cover a broader terrain than all of the SALT agreements. These decisions will play a very important role in determining the framework of international economic justice or injustice in every conceivable dimension of the world economy for both the rich and the poor nations. They will touch everything from the smallest trade package to the out-come of the International Law of the Sea Conference, from conditions for loans to the limits of trade quotas, from development priorities to energy conservation, from the stability of commodity prices to the amounts of development aid, from the rate of industrial growth to the cost of pollu-tion control.

The point of this brief excursion into the contemporary international economy is to show that the "legal formalities" hardly touch questions of economic policy integration. American efforts to encourage the protection of human rights in Uganda or the Soviet Union, or to aid the emergence of majority rule in Southern Africa, or to see that the Soviet Union abides by its treaty commitments, will not, in themselves, lead to substantive economic justice for the peo-ple in Uganda, South Africa, the Soviet Union, Canada, or Japan. Moreover, it is clear that the questions about national sovereignty and the formal independence of states are in-creasingly less urgent in the realm of economic inter-dependence to the point where the most crucial questions now are those that ask about the *kind* of interdependence that will be established; not about *whether* there will be any interdependence.

What do Christians have to offer at this point? Do we believe that economic justice for Latin America and Africa should mean serious curtailment of our own North American pattern of economic growth and an enlargement of foreign aid? If so, how would we argue that case concretely? Do we believe that an increasingly interdependent world should lead to an increasing degree of cooperation and political integra-tion for the sake of public international justice? If so, then how would we propose to transform the powerful influence

of those who want to keep America number one and allow
sufficient independence for them to go their own way, even if
that does not lead to greater justice for others?

Unless we can develop an integral vision of concrete, institutional, public justice on a global scale that can demonstrate its power in handling the details of economic interdependence, military and arms growth, nuclear limitations, health, hunger, and education, then surely we are fail-
ing to develop one of our greatest opportunities and obligations for Christian service. If there is any movement on earth
that should be carrying forward an international, cooperative
effort to achieve global justice, it should be the movement of
the Body of Christ which claims to know, love, and serve the
King of the whole earth. If there is any community that
should be constantly at work trying to demonstrate concrete
political implications of its global responsibilities, it should
be the Christian community. Instead of that visible
manifestation of Christian service, however, we typically find
Christians locked into nationalistic, liberal, and socialist
ideologies that drain the dynamic power from the heart of the
Gospel.

Justice Within and Among States

Up to this point we have argued that Christian responsibility in the realm of international politics can come to expression only if we approach that realm with a sense of the integral, concrete wholeness of political reality at the global
level. The responsibility for normative decision-making on
the part of states is an *integral part* of the international
political *reality*. We have also argued that in order to contribute something substantial and significant to an understanding of the framework within which those normative
decisions will be made, Christians will have to transcend the
limits of the liberal, democratic political vision. We will have
to elaborate a different, more concrete, more institutional,
more material conception of public justice if we want to ad-

53

dress the full reality of international interdependence as it is now emerging.[14]

In the final analysis, therefore, we must, in one sense, both begin and end by resolving the deceptive swindle we examined in our consideration of the realist hypothesis about "immoral states." The most fundamental question, in other words, concerns the nature of the political community, the identity of the state which is not an individual person but which nevertheless acts out its will in the context of some kind of normative responsiveness. And, of course, this is closely intertwined with the question of the identity and unique limits of interstate relations. A final illustrative issue may help us grasp this problem more clearly.

An important study in the 1960s by Johan Galtung[15] described the international political domain as a highly stratified system in which a few "topdog nations" stand at the pinnacle of a hierarchy over a descending order of "underdog" states, each with less power than the state above it. One of the major findings of Galtung's work, as Marshall Singer summarizes it, "is that the less powerful states tend to interact less (or not at all) with each other and more with the powerful states, while powerful states tend to interact more among themselves than they do with weaker states."[16] This means, among other things, that the weakest states have only a very few foreign policy options and are quite dependent upon the more powerful states, while the most powerful states have a very broad range of options and are relatively more independent.

> At every step up the hierarchy, the number of international interactions and foreign policy options increases. The U.S. interacts most with Britain, Canada, and the EEC [European Economic Community], but it also interacts with India, Sri Lanka, and even the Maldive Islands. Conversely, the Maldivians can only interact with the Ceylonese [of Sri Lanka], and even then on a limited rather one-way basis.[17]

One of the important consequences that Galtung's study points out is the detrimental outcome of this arrangement for the poorer and weaker states with respect to their ability to establish communities of real public justice. A small state like Ceylon (now Sri Lanka) is heavily dependent upon its tea for foreign exchange, as is Cuba on sugar. American commercial interests that deal in tea or sugar, however, are obviously only small interests among hundreds of American international enterprises. Likewise, we can see that for all its power, the American army is only one powerful interest in the American government, along with a high-powered navy, air force, state department, labor department, and so forth. By contrast, a very small army in a weak state might be the one institution with overwhelming influence and control.

What happens, then, when the American tea industry decides to carry out a policy in its own interest that puts tremendous pressure on the tea producers of Sri Lanka? The consequences may be practically unfelt and even unnoticed in the United States but earthshaking in Sri Lanka for not only the tea industry, but the whole economy and the public order as well.

Or let us enter the public governmental sphere and take the case of Chile, as Marshall Singer does, realizing that Chile is a stronger and more diversified country than many others. In 1970 Salvador Allende was elected president on a platform of social reform that was to include the nationalization of large American economic interests. The subsequent efforts of ITT to get the American government to intervene directly to overthrow Allende are well established. After the nationalization process got under way, the American government cut off all economic aid to Chile. "What is less well known, however," explains Singer, "is that despite termination of economic aid, the U.S. government *increased* its aid to (and training of) the Chilean military throughout the period of Allende's rule."[18] After nationalization, the American government figured that in the long run its interests might best be served by means of the Chilean military. Allende, of course, did not want to be dependent on that aid from the United States, but he could not cut it off without risking the alienation of the military which was essential for his rule. Ultimately, American military aid to the Chilean military did have the consequences that Allende feared and that the United States desired.[19]

The point is that a fairly small amount of American military influence, which was only one of the government's thousands of foreign policies in operation around the globe at the time, turned out to be a major influence in Chilean politics.

While American citizens enjoy the benefits of a relatively well-developed and stable political system, along with the freedom and diversity of a complex social order, most people in the weaker, smaller states are locked into a relatively confined existence that can be controlled in a very lopsided and unjust fashion by one industry or commodity market, or by a powerful military or very small, relatively wealthy, upper class elite. When the United States throws a small portion of its weight around without due consideration of the possible unjust consequences in states that are not similarly developed, it contributes to injustice internationally as well as in the domestic affairs of the affected countries. And in a parallel fashion, when the American government allows its private, commercial and corporate interests to have free play in the world, even when that free play is powerfully disruptive of public justice in other countries, then the government and its citizens bear some responsibility for the public injustice caused by those private interests.

Our conclusions, therefore, about what will lead to international justice must be built solidly and carefully upon a clear understanding of what public justice ought to be within and among states. If we callously overlook the tremendously significant and complex array of social communities and institutions that need to grow together in a balanced context of public justice in new states, and if we simply assume that what is good for America is good for the rest of the world, then we cannot possibly gain a perspective on international politics that can be called Christian and just.

Precisely at this point our own most serious political weakness in the West produces our blindness as well as our realist/idealist ambivalence. We lack a positive, concrete, normative understanding of what local, national, and international communities of public justice ought to look like. Thus, in the international arena we vacillate back and forth between tough, so-called realistic power plays and idealistic, superficial, altruistic efforts to make the rest of the world safe for democracy and prosperity.

International justice is both a norm and a substantive reality of health and harmony within states and among them. What appears to serve one nation's interests today might not be what is just for everyone in the long run. An amoral realism could make Americans proud and rich today, but it might lead to death and destruction for American grandchildren and their Canadian, Mexican, and Chinese neighbors in the year 2000. Yes, international diplomacy is difficult, uncertain, and not carried out by the unilateral acts of individual states. But the demands for justice remain nonetheless even if nations refuse to heed them. The normative question in nineteenth-century Europe, in the world today, and in the world of tomorrow was, is, and will remain: "What are the nations of the earth doing to achieve justice for all?" And the question comes with the greatest force and the greatest demand to the most powerful nations on earth.

4

Unity and Diversity Among States: Roots of the Western Tradition

Three main cultural streams lie at the root of modern western political life—the Judeao-Christian, the classical Greek, and the Roman stoic. These three were joined together in various ways in the European Middle Ages. Each of these streams had different emphases, and the medieval period was unique in that its emphasis was more than merely the sum of the earlier three parts. In each tradition, however, and in the Middle Ages, there was a very definite conception of the *unity* that should pervade or control the earthly *diversity* of "political" realms.

Biblical Tradition

The Hebraic-Christian tradition presents us with the normative proclamation that the only God, the Creator of all things, is the Ruler of the ends of the earth. The earth is a unity because it belongs, as creation, to the only God. All kings and kingdoms, therefore, exist as servants of God, subject to His ultimate will and purposes.[1] Psalm 2 is a concentrated example of this:

Why do the nations rage
    and the peoples plot in vain?
The kings of the earth take their stand
    and the rulers gather together against the LORD
    and against his Anointed One.
"Let us break their chains," they say,
    "and throw off their fetters."

The One enthroned in heaven laughs;
    the Lord scoffs at them.
Then he rebukes them in his anger
    and terrifies them in his wrath, saying,
"I have installed my King
    on Zion, my holy hill."

I will proclaim the decrees of the LORD:

He said to me, "You are my Son;
    today I have become your Father.
Ask of me,
    and I will make the nations your inheritance,
    the ends of the earth your possession.
You will rule them with an iron scepter;
    you will dash them to pieces like pottery."

Therefore, you kings, be wise;
    be warned, you rulers of the earth.
Serve the LORD with fear
    and rejoice with trembling.
Kiss the Son, lest he be angry
    and you be destroyed in your way,
for his wrath can flare up in a moment.
    Blessed are all who take refuge in him.
                        (New International Version)

For the prophet Isaiah this could only mean that the diverse kings and kingdoms have their existence in order to reveal the glory of God's *one* kingdom, God's unified rule over the whole earth. They are literally at God's disposal; "Before him all the nations are as nothing; they are regarded by him as worthless and less than nothing" (Isaiah 40:17, NIV).

> Do you not know?
> > Have you not heard?
> Has it not been told you from the beginning?
> > Have you not understood since the earth was founded?
> He sits enthroned above the circle of the earth,
> > and its people are like grasshoppers.
> He stretches out the heavens like a canopy,
> > and spreads them out like a tent to live in.
> He brings princes to naught
> > and reduces the rulers of this world to nothing.
> > > (Isaiah 40:21-23, NIV)

The Old Testament revelation about God's universal Kingdom was attached to the historical person and work of Jesus, God's Son, the Christ. Jesus claimed that "all authority in heaven and on earth has been given to me" (Matthew 28:18, RSV). The New Testament letter to the Hebrews picked up Psalm 2 and other passages and argued that the "Son," begotten by the Father, is the Lord and King over all. Other New Testament passages elaborate this further.

Not only did the biblical tradition insist on the rule of God behind and above all earthly dominions, but it pointed ahead, through history, to the eschatological and visible fulfillment of God's reign over all. Kings and rulers, therefore, hold stewardly offices beneath God's rule, and they should use those offices for the sake of divine justice, lest God depose them now and bring them to judgment in the end.

Classical Greek Tradition

In classical Greek thought, particularly that of Plato and Aristotle, the unity of all earthly political orders is to be found in the universal cosmic rhythms that control their birth, growth, and decay. At the same time, however, unity can be discovered in the universal rational form or principle in which each political community participates.[2] The attempts at federation among historical Greek city-states came later,[3]

61

and Plato and Aristotle never considered that option seriously. Consequently, the main contribution of classical Greek thought arises from its movement in two directions: on the one hand, it sought to give an adequate account of the recurring patterns of change to which every particular city-state seemed to be subject; on the other hand, especially in Plato, it sought, by philosophical ascent, to discover the universal, changeless form of true political order that would serve as the paradigm or norm for all particular and changing city-states. While Plato lacked the vision of a personal, transcendent God who revealed His sovereign will and historical purpose through kings, prophets, and eventually His own Son, he nevertheless believed that philosophic *(noetic)* quest could lead to the discovery of the rational, transcendent "city-state of health and goodness" that was not itself of human origin. According to Eric Voegelin, the great theme of Plato's late work the *Laws*

> is the question, whether paradigmatic order will be created by 'god or some man' (624a). Plato answers: 'God is the measure of all things' rather than man (716c); paradigmatic order can be created only by 'the God who is the true ruler of the men who have nous' [reason] (713a); the order created by men who anthromorphically conceive themselves as the measure of all things will be a *stasioteia* rather than a *politeia*, a state of feuding rather than a state of order (715b).[4]

The closest that Plato came to an eschatological vision, according to Voegelin, was in his reinterpretation of the eras of Cronos and Zeus. During the age of Cronos people lived "under the direct guidance of the gods," and later in the age of Zeus, they lived in man-made city-states *(poleis)*. A new age would now have to appear.

> After the unhappy experience with human government in the age of Zeus, the time has now come to imitate by all means life as it was under Cronos; and as we cannot return

to the rule of daimons [gods], we must order our homes and poleis in obedience to the *diamonion*, to the immortal element within us. This something, 'what of immortality is in us,' is the *nous* [intelligent mind] and its ordering *nomos* [rational laws]. The new age, following the ages of Cronos and Zeus, will be the age of Nous.[5]

Whereas for Israel and later for Christians the political disorder and disunity of this age would be overcome by the fulfillment of God's Kingdom, for Plato the disorder would be overcome, if at all, by the full dawn of the age of *Nous*.

Roman Stoic Tradition

Beginning soon after Aristotle in Greece but coming to a more mature development in the early Roman Republic and the later Roman Empire was the ethical-juridical philosophy of stoicism. "To the Stoics," as F. Parkinson reminds us, "the world was a unit, irrespective of the manifold particularisms which it displayed, and an object from which to extract a set of laws."[6] Stoic thought was characterized by a rational quest for the unchanging order of the cosmos and thus it was clearly Greek. But it developed after the city-state declined and when the great empires of Alexander and of the later Romans were emerging. Thus it became increasingly oriented to the ecumenical universality of the world as a whole.

Chrysippus (280-207 B.C.), "who wrote a treatise *On Law* and was the greatest Athenian seminarist of his time," developed the idea of an order of world law that stood above the social and political distinctions that are apparent all around us. In fact, he believed that these distinctions should be reduced to a minimum.

This applied to all states as much as to individuals. Harmony between states was a Stoic ideal and could conceivably be attained if all states were linked together in a system of universal values based on principles of equality. In the Stoic mind, customs varied, but the element of reason which underpinned natural justice was uniform.[7]

In Roman law the stoic mode of thought came to have a tremendous influence, especially in the development of the laws applying to all peoples, the *jus gentium*. The stoic conception of a natural law, *jus naturale*, controlled the reinterpretation of Roman law in the process of applying it to the people who were being integrated into the Roman Empire, but whose own customs and legal traditions were not those of early Rome. The resulting body of legal interpretation was called *jus gentium*—"the law common to all people making up the Roman Empire."[8]

Marcus Tullius Cicero (106-43 B.C.) summarized the stoic philosophy of law, reason, nature, and God in a way that became its classic statement:

> There is in fact a true law—namely, right reason—which is in accordance with nature, applies to all men, and is unchangeable and eternal. By its commands this law summons men to the performance of their duties; by its prohibitions it restrains them from doing wrong. Its commands and prohibitions always influence good men, but are without effect upon the bad. To invalidate this law by human legislation is never morally right, nor is it permissible ever to restrict its operation, and to annul it wholly is impossible . . . It will not lay down one rule at Rome and another at Athens, nor will it be one rule today and another tomorrow. But there will be one law, eternal and unchangeable, binding at all times upon all peoples; and there will be, as it were, one common master and ruler of men, namely God, who is the author of this law, its interpreter, and its sponsor.[9]

As Eric Voegelin points out, the Ciceronian formulation has remained a constant in history "because it is the only elaborate doctrine of law produced by the ecumenic-imperial society."[10] It became the formative force in Roman law, and the early Latin Christian fathers adopted it instead of developing an independent philosophy of law derived from the Hebraic-Christian tradition. "The background of Roman law in the formation of the European lawyers' guilds, and the neo-Stoic movements since the Renaissance, have left us the heritage of a 'higher law' and of 'natural law.' "[11]

Parkinson points to an important tension that gradually emerged in Rome between the ideal of legal universalism in Ciceronian stoicism and the concrete, specific power of the Roman imperial armies. Emperor Marcus Aurelius (A.D. 121-180) displayed this tension. On the one hand is his famous stoic dictum, "My city and country is Rome—as a man it is the world." On the other hand, he believed in the particular freedom of individuals and states. Says Parkinson, "Here was the philosophical frame within which the tragic dilemma of international relations was to pose itself time and again, with the freedom of individual states pitted against the ideal of a preordained universe."[12] The rational, moral, legal universalism of stoic philosophy did not come sufficiently to grips with the reality of diverse, particular, political powers. The idea of a cosmic legal unity that controlled stoic thinking easily transcended the limits of the small Greek city-states, but it apparently did not get very far outside the particularity of the Roman Empire.

The Medieval Tradition

The Christian-Hebraic, Greek, and Roman traditions flowed together during the centuries after Christ. Parkinson summarizes this development quite succinctly:

> Once Christianity had been adopted as the state religion of the Roman Empire at the end of the fourth century A.D., Stoic notions of universality, reinforced by the powerful memory of the Roman imperial structure, were to facilitate the eventual transition from *res publica romana* to *res publica christiana*. It also led to the transformation of Seneca's conception of a universal mankind held together by

universally valid moral ties to the notion of an imperial theocracy imposing a universal dogma binding on rulers and their subjects alike.[13]

The transition from Roman Empire to Holy Roman Empire was not a rapid one, however. The process took centuries. The most important figure during the transition was St. Augustine (A.D. 354-430), and the thinker who best represents the culmination of the process is St. Thomas Aquinas (1225-1274).

Augustine takes the stoic idea of an eternal natural law and identifies it with the eternal law of the biblical God.[14] The special revelation of God to the Jews and through Christ is an explication of the eternal natural law.

> Since natural law or the law of conscience is innate in man, it has existed since the creation of Adam. Therefore, it precedes the Fall and the introduction of sin into the world, and it antedates and is distinguished from the written law given directly by God to the Jews through Moses as well as the law of Christ in the Gospels. The Ten Commandments and the Gospel precepts do not contradict or annul the law of nature; rather, they make it more explicit and overt and give it the greater force of God's direct commandment to men.[15]

A crucial difference between Augustine and the stoics, however, is Augustine's conviction that while *social* life is natural to humans, *political* and *legal* orders are not. The latter are God-given orders designed to restrain sin; they came into existence after the fall into sin. They were not originally part of human nature. The very existence of diverse political entities, therefore, is evidence of the disunity and brokenness of natural society among humans. The recovery of true social life, of true justice, will occur only in the City of God—the eschatological community of God's new people, which is being redeemed by Christ in the midst of this age but which will appear in its completion only after Christ returns to judge the earth. The present age, therefore, can only be an age of relative or limited justice maintained by force in the midst of injustice, war, and disorder. The earthly political orders themselves can never achieve true justice, and an international order of justice in this world would be even more unthinkable.[16]

Augustine manifests a degree of Platonism in his notion that the relative justice and equity that are sometimes achieved on earth are due to the fact that "vestiges," "semblances," and "images" of true justice can still be found in human life on earth. Although earthly peace is different from heavenly peace, it may be thought of as a "blurred image" of the heavenly.[17] But in the final analysis he does not view the City of God as a paradigm of earthly political order. Rather, the earthly political orders are only temporary restraining devices that will finally succumb to the triumph of the City of God which is much more than a city-state or an empire.

Augustine's outlook at this point led him along a different path than the one Plato or the stoics had followed. Augustine was not preoccupied with the philosophical attempt to define the eternal, universal, paradigmatic political order, nor was he preoccupied with the attempt to relativize all particular political differences in the light of an eternal natural law. Moreover, Augustine certainly did not try to justify the Roman Empire's claim to universality. Rather he kept looking beyond the limited political orders, including Rome, toward the Church which he saw as the earthly anticipation of the City of God. The only true unity and universality that Augustine would admit was that of God's reign in Christ.

In the end Augustine was bold enough to argue that *"It concerns Christian kings of this world to wish their mother the Church, of which they have been spiritually born, to have peace in their times."*[18] Since such a wish required action for its fulfillment, Augustine argued ". . . let the kings of the earth serve Christ by making laws for Him and for His cause."[19] The superior authority of the universal Church within this world was not something that Augustine worked out in any great detail as part of a systematic political theory. But the implications of his thinking were worked out both doctrinally and in political fact in Europe during the course of the next one thousand years. At the peak of the High Middle Ages, St. Thomas Aquinas articulated what Augustine had only anticipated but which had in the meantime become the reality of the Christian Roman Empire.

Thomas Aquinas worked out the details of a view of social, political, and religious life that recognized the universal superiority of the Church guiding and integrating the diverse, limited political orders into one *corpus Christianum*, a unified Christian body politic or Christian republic. While weaving together certain Augustinian, stoic, and Platonic themes, Aquinas made much more use of Aristotle in his political theory. Among other things this meant that Aquinas returned to the Greek idea of the naturalness of political life—political orders exist by nature rather than because of sin.

Although Aquinas extends the Aristotelian conception of the city-state to refer to the much larger political realms of his day, he nevertheless maintains the conception of political life as a diversity of limited domains. "There is no open mention, in the whole of St. Thomas's work, of the idea of a universal empire," says A.P. D'Entrèves.

> No doubt the idea of the fundamental unity of mankind is preserved in the general outlines of St. Thomas's conception of politics. It survives in the very notion of a natural law, common to all men, from which the several systems of positive laws derive their substance and value. It survives in the conception of the *unus populus Christianus* [one Christian people], which embraces all countries and nations, and which finds its highest expression in the *Corpus mysticum Ecclesiae* [mystical Church]. But in the sphere of practical politics it is the particular State which carries the day.[20]

For Aquinas, then, it is clear that the unity of political realms or domains is to be found not in some form of political unity *per se* but in the Church's universal embrace of different political orders. In fact, the Church actually functioned at that time as an international legal order within Europe. One of Aquinas' important statements on the relationship between the Church and earthly governments is this:

> We must note that government and dominion depend from human law, but the distinction between the faithful and infidels is from divine law. The divine law, however, which is a law of grace, does not abolish human law which is founded on natural reason. So the distinction between the faithful and the infidel, considered in itself, does not invalidate the government and dominion of infidels over the faithful. Such right to dominion or government may, however, with justice be abrogated by order of the Church in virtue of her divine authority; for the infidel, on account of their unbelief, deserve to lose their power over the faithful, who are become the sons of God. But the Church sometimes does and sometimes does not take such steps.[21]

Whatever the authenticity and permanency of natural law, natural political life, and natural reason, it is clear in Aquinas that the final authority among nations resides in the Church as the divinely appointed channel of unity on earth. Aquinas is willing to recognize political diversity as natural because he sees the ultimate unity among peoples achieved and maintained by a suprapolitical legal authority—the Church.

In the centuries prior to the Renaissance and the Reformation, prior to the appearance of modern states and thinkers such as Machiavelli, we find neither a highly developed conception of the state nor a highly developed conception of interstate relations. What we do find, however, is a strong sense of moral, legal, or rational unity that ought to rule the world. The basic differences in the traditions we have considered come from fundamentally different conceptions of God, of human nature, and of the ultimate purpose of human life on earth. Many of the differences and conflicts among those traditions are still influential in shaping our understanding and our political actions in the contemporary world.

5

Three Contemporary Views of International Unity and Diversity

With the decline of the Holy Roman Empire and the rise of new states, a different kind of international order emerged in the West, one that no longer reflected the theories of Aquinas, Augustine, Cicero, or Plato. Figures such as Hugo Grotius, Immanuel Kant, G.W.F. Hegel, and Napoleon Bonaparte were conscious of this fact, and each tried in his own way to reinterpret or to rebuild world unity out of its newly emerging fragmentation. It is the modern world of supposedly self-determining, sovereign states that we know from experience today. In this chapter we will try to uncover some of the assumptions that several political scientists hold about the unity and diversity of states today. We will also look for influences from ancient perspectives on these contemporary interpretations of international relations.

The Modern Realism of Hans J. Morgenthau

Hans J. Morgenthau is perhaps best known for the many editions of his text, *Politics Among Nations*. In 1970 he published a collection of essays, including some of his best philosophical ones, entitled *Truth and Power*.[1] One of the essays in this book, "On Trying to be Just," first published in 1963, shows that Morgenthau's thinking is a secularized agnostic version of Augustine's ideas. Human nature is fundamentally faulty in a moral sense, according to Morgenthau, and for this reason anything like a just state or a just world order is simply out of the question.

> Justice, immortality, freedom, power, and love—those are the poles that attract and thereby shape the thoughts and actions of men. They have one quality in common that constitutes the distinction of men from beasts and gods alike: Achievement falls short of aspiration . . .
>
> Man alone is, as it were, suspended between heaven and earth: an ambitious beast and a frustrated god. For he alone is endowed with the faculty of rational imagination that outpaces his ability to achieve . . . His freedom is marred by the power of others, as his power is by their freedom.[2]

But whereas Augustine's pessimism about sinful human nature was controlled by his faith in the ultimate will and purpose of God in Christ, Morgenthau's pessimism is qualified only by agnosticism. Even if we assume that justice is a reality, argues Morgenthau, "we are incapable of realizing it" and incapable of knowing what it demands. He says:

> The position we are taking here has the advantage, at least for cognitive purposes, that it coincides with the one men have always taken because they could not do otherwise. Men have always thought and acted *as though* justice were real. We are proceeding here on the same assumption, trying to show that, even if justice is real, man cannot achieve it for reasons that are inherent in his nature. The reasons are three: Man is too ignorant, man is too selfish, and man is too poor.[3]

Morgenthau is working here with what we might call a "negative universality" in his conception of both human nature and political reality. He puts forth a thesis that few would attempt to deny, namely, that human creatures manifest selfishness, ignorance, and poverty. But this thesis appears to be a "self-evident truth" only because of the historical backdrop of modern relativistic cynicism and skepticism regarding the norms that the ancient traditions believed could be known. If we did not have firm roots in traditions that established norms of "unselfishness," 'knowledge," and "richness" of human life, we would not be able to be so *certain* now about the opposites or negations of those norms. Morgenthau's "agnosticism," in other words, has an eerie sense of "certainty" about it; he *knows* with certainty an awful lot about what we cannot know with any certainty. Counting on the fact that most of his readers will be skeptical agnostic relativists, he can depend on their agreement with him that injustice can be recognized without having any sure knowledge of what justice is, that selfishness can be known without being sure of what unselfishness is.

> In sum, our knowledge of what justice demands is predicated upon our knowledge of what the world is like and what it is for, of a hierarchy of values reflecting the objective order of the world. Of such knowledge, only theology can be certain, and secular philosophies can but pretend to have it.
>
> However, even theology can have that knowledge only in the abstract and is as much at a loss as are secular philosophies when it comes to applying abstract principles to concrete cases.[4]

As we saw in the last chapter, Augustine located true justice in the City of God and for that reason he never adequately accounted for its relationship to earthly political life. In that sense his "theology" was too abstract in Morgenthau's terms. But Morgenthau simply affirms the abstract Augustinian separation of justice from the real world without explaining why he has dismissed the City of God from his consideration. With assured certainty that his readers in the modern age will not resort to any of the ancient moral arguments, Morgenthau can dispense with considerations of "justice" for all practical purposes, even if he allows that justice might exist beyond our knowledge or ability to realize it. Then he moves forward confidently with the primary thrust of his negation, that is, his belief that human creatures are *universally* self-deceptive and selfish. Moreover, he assumes that this universal condition of humans essentially explains international political behavior.[5] Without any doubt about the universality of his claims, Morgenthau argues that,

> All of us look at the world and judge it from the vantage point of our interests. We judge and act as though we were at the center of the universe, as though what we see everybody must see, and as though what we want is legitimate in the eyes of justice . . . This propensity for self-deception is mitigated by man's capacity for transcending himself, for trying to see himself as he might look to others. This capacity, however feeble and ephemeral it may be, is grounded in man's rational nature, which enables him to understand himself and the world around him with a measure of objectivity. Yet where rational objective knowledge is precluded from the outset, as it is with justice, the propensity for self-deception has free rein. As knowledge restrains self-deception, so ignorance strengthens it. Since man cannot help but judge and act in terms of justice and since he cannot know what justice requires, but since he knows for sure what he wants, he equates with a vengeance his vantage point and justice. Empirically we find, then, as many conceptions of justice as there are vantage points, and the absolute majesty of justice dissolves into the reality of so many interests and points of view.[6]

The consequence of this argument is that both the human quest for a normative understanding of true justice as well as human receptivity to God's revelation are excluded without exception (i.e., universally) from the realm of politics, if not from life altogether. The only *reality* in political life, as Morgenthau sees it, is the self-interested quest for power, and that reality is truly universal, not as a norm but as a natural fact.[7] Thus Morgenthau would overcome the tension that existed between stoic universalism and Roman imperial expansionism by eliminating the former from consideration. The autonomous freedom of particular states is the *only* international reality. In this sense, Morgenthau responds to those who would criticize as immoral and unjust the post-World War II struggle between the United States and the Soviet Union to secure "spheres of influence" in the rest of the world by saying,

> Spheres of influence, as Churchill and Stalin knew and Roosevelt recognized sporadically, have not been created by evil and benighted statesmen and, hence, cannot be abolished by an act of will on the part of good and enlightened ones. Like the balance of power, alliances, arms races, political and military rivalries and conflicts, and the rest of "power politics," spheres of influence are the ineluctable by-product of the interplay of interests and power in a society of sovereign nations.[8]

The only way to stop the struggle for spheres of influence is to change the world from one of competing sovereign states to one where a single "sovereign government can set effective limits to the expansionism of the nations composing it."[9] This suggestion for global politics, though Morgenthau does not argue for it at this point, is an enlarged version of Thomas Hobbes' answer to the domestic power struggle among competing individuals. Only Leviathan, a giant power, can put an end to the minipower struggle.[10]

Since international politics is essentially a power struggle, no predictive or normative theory of international relations is possible, according to Morgenthau.[11] The only "unifying" factor in interstate relations is the universality of the power struggle. But the fact of the struggle implies that unpredictable competitive diversities will rule the world until a single world organization of power is attained—something which itself cannot be predicted. Some of the new post-war theorists of international relations are not really offering "theories," says Morgenthau; they are simply putting forward new dogmas of their own construction. "They do not so much try to reflect reality as it actually is as to superimpose upon a recalcitrant reality a theoretical scheme that satisfies the desire for thorough rationalization. Their practicality is specious, since it substitutes what is desirable for what is possible."[12]

A new era of international relations theory does not exist in fact, but only in rhetoric or in hope. The distinctive quality of politics is the struggle for power, and just as this struggle is morally repellant to Christians, it is intellectually unsatisfactory to theorists because power, like love,

> is a complex psychological relationship that cannot be completely dissolved into a rational theoretical scheme. The theoretician of international relations who approaches his subject matter with respect for its intrinsic nature will find himself frustrated morally, politically, and intellectually; for his aspiration for a pervasively rational theory is hemmed in by the insuperable resistance of the subject matter.
>
> The new theories of international relations have yielded to the temptation to overcome this resistance of the subject matter by disregarding its intrinsic nature.[13]

Does this mean, then, that international relations cannot be studied in any fruitful theoretical manner? Does it mean that the contingent, unpredictable behavior of autonomous states will yield no theoretical generalizations? No, Morgenthau does not want to come to that conclusion. Instead, what he proposes is that the right kind of reflection on the actual history of international relations can help "to bring order and meaning into a mass of unconnected material and to increase knowledge through the logical development of certain propositions empirically established."[14]

But how is this possible? Did not Morgenthau contend that the struggle for power is not amenable to "intellectual ordering"? Can one develop logical propositions on the basis of the empirical struggle for power? Morgenthau's answer is that while a final and complete predictive theory of international relations is impossible, nevertheless, if we see political theory from the standpoint of its practical function within a relatively limited "political environment," then we will be able to see that a theoretical clarification of different practical political alternatives is indeed possible.[15]

> Edmund Burke is a typical example of how great and fruitful political theory develops from concrete practical concerns. It is not being created by a professor sitting in his ivory tower and, with his publisher, looking over a contract that stipulates the delivery of a manuscript on the "theory of International Relations" by a specified date. It is developed out of the concern of a politically alive and committed mind with the concrete political problems of the day. Thus, all the great political theory, from Plato and Aristotle and the Biblical prophets to our day, has been practical political theory that intervenes actively in a concrete political situation with the purpose of change through action.[16]

Clearly, then, Morgenthau's agnosticism with respect to the normative considerations of justice as well as with respect to modern scientific theories of social behavior is not a *total* agnosticism. His estimate of the ignorance, poverty, and selfishness of human creatures is not *completely* pessimistic. While giving up the Platonic and biblical convictions that universal justice can be known, he nevertheless holds on to the hope that some "practical wisdom" can be gained for life in this world. While rejecting the modern social a-scientific pseudo-hope of achieving a complete empirical theory, Morgenthau nevertheless believes that historical empirical evidence can yield some generalizations of a practical sort that are relatively universal. Morgenthau's skepticism about human nature is not total; the practical wisdom of a few realistic men in this world can transcend the almost universal

77

ignorance, selfishness, and poverty of humankind.[17]

Thus Morgenthau lives with the problems of the international power struggle not as a man without any knowledge or hope, but as one who is dismayed only by the normative moralist and by the pseudoscientific system builder. If we could do away with those who believe that they know what justice is and with those who hope that they can predict with certainty what will happen in the future, then we could begin to have real confidence in the practical theory of the Hans Morgenthaus of this world. In fact, the ultimate task that a Morgenthau-style theory can perform, argues the author, "is to prepare the ground for a new international order radically different from that which preceded it."[18] How, we might ask, can a practical theory devoid of any ultimate moral norm as well as of predictive powers nevertheless prepare the ground for a new world order? It does so, according to Morgenthau, because the rational powers of the practical theorist can "anticipate" the future on the basis of past experience. The political power struggle is sufficiently universal and repetitive that logical extrapolation from past circumstances, which takes into account new technologies such as nuclear weapons, can foretell and lead into the future even without being able to predict it.

> It is a legitimate and vital task for a theory of politics to anticipate drastic changes in the structure of politics and in the institutions which must meet a new need. The great political utopians have based their theoretical anticipation of a new political order upon the realistic analysis of the empirical *status quo* in which they lived. Today, political theory and, more particularly, a theory of international relations, starting from the understanding of politics and international relations as they are, must attempt to illuminate the impact nuclear power is likely to exert upon the structure of international relations and upon the functions domestic government performs. Further, it must anticipate in a rational way the intellectual, political, and institutional changes that this unprecedented revolutionary force is likely to require.[19]

Karl W. Deutsch's Analysis of International Relations

While Morgenthau is skeptical of both the moralist and the scientific system builder, he is still hopeful about the potential of a practical political theory that can guide the actions of real statesmen in real states toward a new international order. Karl Deutsch, on the other hand, is the kind of scientist that Morgenthau would criticize for attempting the impossible—that is, attempting to rationalize or systematize in an almost natural scientific fashion a reality that cannot be so reduced. Deutsch's assumptions are clear and simple in their reductionistic disregard of human political and moral reality and its integral complexity. He is much more than an agnostic when it comes to considerations of "justice," "morality," and "truth." Deutsch's view of human nature and the world is that of a closed universe manifesting stimulus-response actions and reactions based on the struggle for satisfaction and survival against pain and death. True justice is not merely unknowable; it is an irrelevant matter in the context of a scientific examination of the "facts."

What governments do, says Deutsch, is to "pursue their goals in either a conscious or a machine-like fashion."[20] The term "goal" in this sentence should be defined as follows, according to Deutsch:

> A *goal* (*goal state* [condition]) for any acting system is that state of affairs, particularly in its relationship to the outside world, within which its inner disequilibrium—its drive—has been reduced to a relative minimum. If a state is in some sort of disequilibrium or tension—and most states, like most other acting systems, are in some disequilibrium of this kind —it will tend to change some aspects of its behavior until this disequilibrium is reduced.[21]

If this quotation gives the reader an initial impression that Deutsch is working with abstract physical, mechanical, or psychological concepts that do not explain the full and integral reality of human political life, it is a justifiable impression. Repeatedly Deutsch makes use of physical, mathematical, or mechanical illustrations in order to render his analysis of political life. For example:

> The making of foreign policy thus resembles a pinball machine game. Each interest group, each agency, each important official, legislator, or national opinion leader, is in the position of a pin, while the emerging decision resembles the end-point of the path of a steel ball bouncing down the board from pin to pin. Clearly, some pins will be placed more strategically than others, and on the average they will thus have a somewhat greater influence on the outcome of the game. But no one pin will determine the outcome. Only the distribution of all the relevant pins on the board—for some or many pins may be so far out on the periphery as to be negligible—will determine the distribution of outcomes. This distribution often can be predicted with fair confidence for large numbers of runs, but for the single run—as for the single decision—even at best only some probability can be stated.[22]

One need not read too far into Deutsch, therefore, to discover that the "unity" which holds the field of disparate political facts together is the unifying concept of the "system"—an unqualified and highly abstract general concept that is used to describe any complex set of interactions. Unity and diversity among states, for Deutsch, has nothing to do with divine sovereignty over our *one* world or with universal moral or political principles that can be discerned by a common rational quest. If there is any unity in the political world, Deutsch believes that it is to be found in the universal mechanical necessity of interactions within a system where equilibrium is pursued and disequilibrium is avoided. It is a unity to be abstracted by use of the proper scientific tools of measurement that can "cut into" the vast array of facts.[23]

What makes Deutsch so interesting in connection with the theme of international unity and diversity is that his method and approach to the subject matter of international relations keep him from adequately answering three very important questions that he poses at the beginning of his book. Of twelve fundamental questions that he asks, the first two are concerned precisely with the unity and diversity among states.

1. *Nation and World:* What are the relations of a nation to the world around it? When, how, and how quickly are a people, a state, and a nation likely to arise, and when, how, and how quickly are they apt to disappear? While they last, how do they relate to other peoples, states, and nations? How do they deal with smaller groups within them, and with individuals, and how do they relate to international organizations and to the international political system?

2. *Transnational Processes and International Interdependence:* To what extent can the governments and peoples of any nation-state decide their own future, and to what extent does the outcome of their actions depend on conditions and events outside their national boundaries? Are the world's countries and nations becoming more "sovereign" and independent from each other, or are they becoming more interdependent in their actions and their fate? Or are they becoming both more independent and more interdependent, but in different sectors of activity? What will the world look like in, say, A.D. 2010 in regard to these matters?[24] The fifth question that he poses is perhaps the most important preliminary one for the scientist or theorist: "What is political in international relations, and what is not? What is the relation of international politics to the life of the society of nations?"[25]

The problem in Deutsch's presentation is that his questions are confined dogmatically to the "hows" that might possibly yield empirical descriptions and measurements. He does not ask about the "whys" and "oughts" or about the conditioning assumptions that guide his investigation of the "hows." Moreover, after raising the questions, his first step is to adopt a concept of "system" that is too abstract and general to serve as a sufficient "tool" for selecting and collecting information about specifically *political* "facts." Only after he has defined what a "system" is, in general, does he begin to define politics, but at that point the full reality of political life can no longer be grasped or contained in his reduced concept of "system." Thus, his fifth question is never answered satisfactorily.

It is legitimate, of course, to ask the present critic to explain what he means by his accusation that Deutsch's system-concept is reductionistic and therefore faulty. In his writings, Deutsch shows great dependency on the work of Norbert Wiener, the mathematician and cybernetic theorist, and Talcott Parsons, a sociological systems theorist.[26] From Parsons he obtains an idea of the social system—unqualified in any specific way. Deutsch accepts Parson's conclusion that "there are certain fundamental things that must be done in every social system, large or small (that is, in every group, every organization, every country) if it is to endure."[27] The things that must be done by a social system include (1) maintaining itself, (2) adapting itself to change, (3) attaining its goals, and (4) integrating its own internal and complex diversity. The scientific key to getting at the functions of any social system, according to Deutsch, is to map the "flow" of the system's communication network which functions as a cybernetic web within the system, and which also connects it with its external environment.

It should be clear to any social scientist that Deutsch, following Wiener and Parsons, has indeed abstracted certain dimensions, modes, or functions of universality that characterize any social entity. It is hard to object to Deutsch's conclusion that *all* social entities seek to maintain their identities, adapt to change, maintain a flow of communication, and so forth. The fundamental problem, however, is that the study of any particular *mode* or *function* of a social system *presupposes* the system's *identity* as a social whole. Deutsch does not indicate an awareness of this, and as a consequence he tends to reduce the political (or any other) system to its communication patterns or to its general functions without explaining *what* it is that is thus functioning or processing information. Instead of first accounting for *what* is political and then carefully examining the abstracted communication flows, Deutsch works backward in a typical reductionistic fashion by first positing an abstract, general social or cybernetic system and then using that abstraction to identify policital life and processes. The effect is to reduce the integral reality of political life to one or two of its modes or functions.[28]

Furthermore, even though Deutsch is not claiming to say anything normative with this approach, he nevertheless believes that a political system that suffers a communication breakdown, or disappears, or fails to adapt quickly to change, or fails to attain its goals, or remains disorganized, is not living up to the universal necessity of survival and development which is incumbent upon all systems, by definition. In other words, it is not doing what it *ought* to do if it wants to survive and grow. The conceptual tool of "system" thus enables the theorist to do more than simply describe facts; it also helps him to make judgments about successful and unsuccessful systems based on the analyst's predisposition to believe that things (including social things) *ought* to survive rather than perish.

Every social system is defined by the above abstraction, in Deutsch's view. What, then, is a "political system" as distinguished from a non-political system? Deutsch is not any more helpful than Morgenthau at this point. Each man more or less assumes that by common sense we are acquainted with "laws" and "forces" which define states or "nation-states."[29] Morgenthau moves on from that point to work with an assumed macrocosmic "person" or "actor" known as the state or political system which seeks, (or should seek), to maintain and enhance its own self-interest. The nominalistic and behavioralistic Deutsch does not so readily admit to the existence of a structured social "whole." Instead, his "political system" is a pattern of combined individual behavior patterns. "*Politics* consists in the more or less incomplete control of human behavior through voluntary habits of *compliance* in combination with threats of probable *enforcement*. In its essence, politics is based on the interplay of habits of cooperation as modified by threats."[30]

Deutsch does not stop to address the objections that might be raised by those who do not accept his assumptions. He does not ask whether the individual habits preceded and helped to shape the particular contours of the political system or whether, to the contrary, they were created by the system. He does not ask why such systems came into existence in the variety of shapes and sizes in which we find them. He does not defend himself against the charge that the above definition no more defines a *political* system than it defines a family, a school, or a business enterprise, since all social systems depend on voluntary compliance and the use of some kinds of enforceable threats. Deutsch goes on to talk about "law," but he does not distinguish state (political) law from church law or school rules or business regulations for employees. In other words, the very thing that needs to be accounted for, namely, the identity of the political system, is passed over rather quickly with some statements about behavior patterns. If this seems inadequate or peculiar, it is so only for the person who is looking for something more than measurements of, and probability predictions about, certain functions carried out by existing domestic and international habits of political behavior.

By the time we reach the concluding sections of Deutsch's *Analysis of International Relations* where he discusses international interdependence and interrelationships, we find nothing that contributes additional insight into the question of the unity and diversity among states. The *diversity* of states is simply assumed to exist as a fact of modernity. The *unity* that he looks for is the universality of shared system properties and the growing complexity of system interdependencies that would seem to require change in the future if the many separate state systems and the world as a whole are to survive.

Once again, without first accounting for the identity of interstate political relationships (as compared with the identity of a state), Deutsch simply assumes the validity and sufficiency of a general systems concept for analyzing international relations. He introduces Chapter Fifteen, "Integration: International and Supranational," this way:

> To *integrate* generally means to make a whole out of parts—that is, to turn previously separate units into components of a coherent system. The essential characteristic of any *system*, we may recall, is a significant degree of interdependence among its components, and *interdependence* between any two components or units consists in the probability that a change in one of them—or an operation performed upon one of them—will produce a predictable change in the other . . .
>
> *Integration*, then, is a relationship among units in which they are mutually interdependent and jointly produce system properties which they would separately lack.[31]

When Deutsch takes up a discussion of the United Nations, he explicitly refers to "two themes" that can be traced throughout the history of that organization: "the search for centralizing power" and "the search for pluralistic communication and accommodation."[32] In other words, the very identity of the United Nations is connected with the problem of *unity* and *diversity* in global politics. Deutsch makes the judgment that a true unification of the world by means of a greater centralization of world political power in the United Nations is not likely to happen in the near future. But, he is willing to follow the suggestion of a "second way" made by Senator Arthur Vandenberg in 1945.

> It is to make the United Nations the town meeting of the world, where all issues can be brought out into the open, and where governments can learn how to manage differences of interest and ideology, and how to avoid head-on

collisions . . . In these respects, the United Nations since 1945 has been remarkably successful.[33]

Almost unrelated to his "scientific" study of communication flows and system functions, and certainly without adequate historical evidence or argument, Deutsch voices his hope for the eventual attainment of world security and unity. His expression of hope seems to be rooted in nothing more than his belief that human beings, when forced up against the wall, will find a way to survive rather than perish. Deutsch believes that somehow a "fit" system will appear that can survive.

> An era of pluralism and, at best, of pluralistic security communities, may well characterize the near future. In the long term, however, the search for integrated political communities that command both peace and power, and that entail a good deal of amalgamation, is likely to continue until it succeeds. For such success, not only good will and sustained effort, but political creativity and inventiveness will be needed, together with a political culture of greater international openness, understanding, and compassion.
> Without such a new political climate and new political efforts, humanity is unlikely to survive for long. But the fact that so many people in so many countries are becoming aware of the problem, and of the need for increasing efforts to deal with it, makes it likely that it will be solved.[34]

Unfortunately, Deutsch contributes little or nothing to our understanding of how compassion, openness, understanding, inventiveness, and political creativity can be found and nurtured. He offers no explanation of why these ingredients will be or should be desired and sought after by the same human beings that Hans Morgenthau believes are all too ignorant, selfish, and poor. One is even left wondering whether Deutsch and Morgenthau, who share so many characteristics of the same culture, language, and political culture, understand each other.[35]

Koehane and Nye: Complex Interdependence

Robert O. Keohane and Joseph S. Nye are fully aware of both Morgenthau's realism and Deutsch's more general and abstract systemic analysis. The thesis of their book, *Power and Interdependence*, is that a more sophisticated approach to the study of world politics is necessary today that can take into account the partial truthfulness of both realism and various forms of systems analysis. Neither "modernists" (a term that would characterize Deutsch in several respects[36]) nor "traditionalists" (the Morgenthaus) have an adequate framework for understanding contemporary international politics, according to Keohane and Nye.

> Modernists point correctly to the fundamental changes now taking place, but they often assume without sufficient analysis that advances in technology and increases in social and economic transactions will lead to a new world in which states, and their control of force, will no longer be important. Traditionalists are adept at showing flaws in the modernist vision by pointing out how military interdependence continues, but find it very difficult accurately to interpret today's multidimensional economic, social, and ecological interdependence.[37]

In contrast to Morgenthau's traditionalism, Keohane and Nye argue that states are not "persons" with single "wills" confronting each other as military powers with a single overriding national interest.[38] States are interdependent not merely as potential military allies or enemies but also as economic, social, and ecological entities. Moreover, many international relationships are of a non-governmental character, and these many "complex interdependencies" are not always organized within each state as parts of a fully integrated, hierarchically arranged, coherent plan of self-interested state action. "In the Canadian-American relationship, for example, the use or threat of force is virtually excluded from consideration by either side. The fact that Canada has less military strength than the United States is therefore not a major factor in the bargaining process."[39] And if we consider American-Canadian relations apart from military interdependence, we discover that there is not a single or uniform "national interest" on each side. The interdependence is more complex than the realist would imagine.

But it is not possible to assume with the "modernist" that the complex interdependence of states within a shrinking global "system" can simply be taken for granted as a single-system fact that will yield empirical measurements of interactions within "the system." The concept of "system" must be used with more agility if we are to be able to take into account both the many different kinds of systemic interdependencies in the world as well as the ways in which systems themselves can change.

In the main body of the book Keohane and Nye examine two major issues and two interstate relationships: international monetary systems and ocean regimes from World War I to 1976, and American-Canadian and American-Australian relations also over a significant period of time. They seek to demonstrate from these analyses that there is no single model of a "system" that can be used to explain either the changes of "regimes" in money and oceans or the changes in bilateral relations between the United States and Canada and between the United States and Australia. In fact, in certain cases, the older realist framework comes the closest to providing an adequate account of the circumstances and events being considered. "Our conclusion is that the traditional tools need to be sharpened and supplemented with new tools, not discarded."[40]

What we find in Keohane and Nye, then, is a more systems-analytical, multi-dimensional, functionalistic, and prediction-oriented approach than in Morgenthau. At the same time, however, the authors display a sensitivity to, and a concern for, the policy-oriented, practical, and historical sides of international politics that are the primary concern of the realists. Given this breadth and complexity, what do Keohane and Nye assume about the unity and diversity among states?

On the basis of *Power and Interdependence* it is difficult to answer this question. In one respect, Keohane and Nye are only testing a few limited hypotheses about the predictive power of certain methods and theoretical approaches, and therefore they end their book with a series of qualifying statements suggesting the necessity of further research rather than with a series of general conclusions that would more clearly reveal their standpoint. In another respect, however, their book makes a case for the severe limits that must be faced in a scientific study of international politics because the closer they get to an account of all the elements of complex interdependence the farther away they stand from any ability to produce clean predictive conclusions. This seems to imply that Keohane and Nye might want to examine the assumptions of contemporary theorists rather carefully since they are calling into question some of their methods and conclusions. Nevertheless, Keohane and Nye do not follow a path of critical reflection on the basic assumptions of international theorists. Instead, they appear to call merely for greater empirical completeness within the framework of assumptions that the traditionalists and the modernists already make. At the conclusion of the book the authors return to a note sounded at its beginning; they want to synthesize and enlarge traditional and modernist contributions in the direction of greater empirical completeness. Traditional views, on the one hand:

> fail even to focus on much of the relevant foreign policy agenda—those areas that do not touch the security and autonomy of the state. Moreover, the policy maxims derived from such traditional wisdom will often be inappropriate. Yet the modernists who believe that social and economic interdependence have totally changed the world fail to take

elements of continuity into account. As a result, their policy prescriptions often appear to be utopian. All four of our cases confirmed a significant role, under some conditions, for the overall military power structure. Appropriate policies must take into account both continuity and change; they must combine elements of the traditional wisdom with new insights about the politics of interdependence.[41]

Thus, Keohane and Nye stand precisely where Morgenthau and Deutsch stand with regard to basic assumptions about the unity and diversity among states. On the one hand, they simply accept as a fact of modernity the existence of separate states without attempting to define the identity of a state. And with Morgenthau and Deutsch they are looking to empirical theorists to come up with an adequate understanding of changing world conditions in order to help states, (and humanity), survive. They want to point out the growing significance of the universal ecological, technological, economic interdependencies among states that function as limiting global necessities which those states ought to acknowledge. But there seems to be no hint in Keohane and Nye that they are interested in reopening the older normative debates about what kind of justice or equity or unity *ought* to characterize the world in its diverse interdependence. They are quite willing to remain entirely agnostic with regard to the normative obligations that states, statesmen, and international organizations have for one another and for the creation in which we all live. Although they, with Morgenthau and Deutsch, want to see into the future, they are skeptical about all forms of foreknowing other than scientific prediction.

If Keohane and Nye are more exhaustive than Morgenthau in their empirical examinations, they are, nevertheless, realists at heart who want to provide nonutopian help to policymakers. If they are less optimistic and less reductionistic than Deutsch because they pay careful attention to actual institutions, historical developments, and complex system changes, they are, nevertheless, systems analysts who limit themselves to the study of the functional relationships among states—especially the developed Western states. They do not leave the positivistic terrain to reflect on and evaluate the assumptions that have guided states and statesmen who have created the modern institutions and regimes. Thus they have no apparatuses, no criteria for assessing and judging the various normative "visions" that statesmen have worked with during the past several centuries of nationalism, imperialism, anti-colonialism, and neo-colonialism. They merely fall back on the rather simplistic distinction between realism and utopianism hoping to avoid the latter at all costs.

The closest that Keohane and Nye come to a recognition of international political norms is when they conclude that political scientists must give greater attention to international *organizations* and *leadership*.

> Our analysis implies that more attention should be paid to the effect of government policies on international regimes. A policy that adversely affects or destroys a beneficial international regime may be unwise, even if its immediate, tangible effects are positive. Concern with maintenance and development of international regimes leads us to pay more attention to problems of *leadership* in world politics. What types of international leadership can be expected, and how can sufficient leadership be supplied? And focus on contemporary world leadership stimulates increased attention to problems of *international organization*, broadly defined.[42]

But even here it is apparent that Keohane and Nye do not attempt to define either "adverse" or "positive" effects, nor do they explain what a "beneficial" international regime would be. And their questions about leadership are the positivistic ones about "what might be expected" and what is "sufficient" without considering what leadership ought to be or even what "sufficiency" means.

Conclusion

What we have in the writings of Morgenthau, Deutsch, Keohane and Nye should not be underestimated, nor should their approaches and findings be dismissed lightly because of their inadequacies. Global relations among states are so complex, so rapidly changing, and so resistant to scientific analysis and measurement that we should not be surprised or disappointed in finding only limited insights and highly tentative conclusions. Instead, we ought to try to understand how the contributions of these thinkers can be used to develop a more encompassing and adequate philosophy and science of international politics.

In spite of his agnosticism, we find in Morgenthau an appreciation for at least two crucial things. First, his realism, for all of its shortcomings, takes its point of departure from an awareness of the integrated *identity-structure of the state*. There is *not* a *similar structural identity in interstate relations*. Morgenthau has not brought this awareness to the forefront of his attention, but his disdain for the abstract system builders who ignore the fact that states act as integral wholes, reveals his keen historical insight into a fundamental feature of the modern global arena. The *first* task of the political scientist, then, is to clarify the identity-structure of the modern state, and do so in a way that illuminates the important similarities and differences between the newer and older states—between complex, highly developed and simpler, less integrated public entities. And along with this task goes the problem of distinguishing interstate relations from intrastate activities. Morgenthau is certainly correct that military power is crucial at this point, but Deutsch and Keohane and Nye are also correct in pointing to the other complex dimensions of interstate relations today.

Second, Morgenthau is aware of the importance of *practical political knowledge*. That is to say, he is conscious that international relations are shaped by real persons making concrete decisions in their political offices on the basis of judgments about what ought to be done to secure peace or prosperity, to preserve peace or to end war, to advance "justice" or to promote certain interests. Keohane and Nye show their dependence on Morgenthau when they, too, indicate the importance of understanding "leadership." An analysis of international relations that does not seek to explain and evaluate this "moral," "judgment-making," "decision-making," human dimension of international politics, but only tries to measure quantities, is an analysis that will not come closer to an exact science, but will only distort more thoroughly the very reality of politics. The *second* task of political science, then, is to reconsider, through critical reflection, the proper assumptions that are necessary to allow for a fully empirical examination of international politics—"fully empirical" meaning the full reality of relationships that are human, institutional, moral, juridical, and social in character. To continue refining natural scientific, cybernetic, mathematical, and other models that simply continue the process of abstracting modes and functions from the integral totality of international politics, is to continue a dogmatically blind effort rather than to advance empirical science.

We find in Deutsch, in contrast to Morgenthau, however, an awareness of some of *the universal modes or dimensions of social structural identities* that can be abstracted from real states and actual interstate relations. Deutsch's specialty, of course, is the study of communications systems and networks. International relations are not simply the "free" and autonomous relations among separate states in an open field. Especially in the last one hundred years, with the advance of modern technologies, communications systems, and worldwide military and economic interdependencies, a more interrelated "global village" testifies to the rise and triumph of the West. It is important then to consider the universal social modes and functions that characterize all states and interstate relations and which limit the more individualistic quests for national self-interest on the part of particular states. Quantification procedures which can help to make us more fully conscious of these universal characteristics should not be ignored or rejected simply because they are reductionistic. They should be employed carefully in the context of a larger, more adequate, non-reductionistic science of politics. The fact that Deutsch has only abstracted some functional elements of social systems, ignoring moral, juridical, aesthetic, historical, and other modes of political existence, as well as almost obliterating the very identity-structure of state, should not lead us to reject entirely the information that he has accumulated or the methods by which he has done so. The *third* task of political science, therefore, must be the careful analysis of all the functional modes of existence that characterize state and interstate political, and nonpolitical system functions. If this objective is pursued in the context of the first two tasks mentioned above, then the work of Deutsch and others can be mined with value, even if with only minimal results.

In Keohane and Nye we can recognize the contribution of theorists who are becoming empirically careful to the point of almost complete tentativeness in the face of the massive complexity of factual international political relations. The fact that the time period for their historical considerations is less than a century, and that their subjects of investigation are the limited issues of money, oceans, American-Canadian, and American-Australian relations, demonstrates the narrow focus that is necessary when scientists attempt to do justice to the full complexity of international politics. Such humility and narrowness must be appreciated and imitated by those who wish to do justice to social science. Even a large team of scientists cannot simply study the international political system in general. The several different models used for their investigations should be analyzed carefully by those who wish to advance the study of international relations. The *fourth* task of political science, then, should be to test hypotheses and assumptions carefully against actual cases over time in order to see whether all of the elements of political reality are being taken into account. The problem with Keohane and Nye does not seem to be so much with a lack of carefulness in what they do, but rather with the systems-analytical assumptions and methods of measurement that circumscribe their project from the outset in a way that hides from view the full integrality of political life.

If it is possible for us to bring together some of the theoretical efforts of Morgenthau, Deutsch, Keohane and Nye into a larger political scientific project, it should also be clear by this point that such a project will have to be much grander than a "picky" eclecticism or an attempted synthesis of existing contributions. In fact, at this point the discussion of the previous chapter should be recalled.

The contemporary world of international relations along with the general moral disposition of scientists in the West is of relatively recent origin. The fact that Morgenthau, Deutsch, Koehane and Nye are all essentially moral and religious agnostics or skeptics when it comes to human "knowing" and "doing," and the fact that the highest moral value they can allow to enter their scientific work is "survival"—these facts mean that the biggest questions of political concern to humanity now and for the last few millenia are being side-stepped by political scientists. The most fundamental question of all, namely, what kind of *unity*, if any, ought to characterize international political diversity is left untouched by the very persons who supposedly know the most about the "new world" that is emerging. The general tenor of their work, however, is not actually one of empty ignorance about this question as though they could really ignore principled questions and stick to a "purely scientific" description of the facts. Instead they are constantly involved in attempts to fill the void by careful qualifications and negations. They must frequently refer to the uselessness of moralists, or to the danger of utopian thinking, or to the necessity of avoiding nuclear war, or to the value of cooperation for world economic growth, or to the importance of system-maintenance. The unity they want is a world unity sufficient to keep most, (or at least enough), humans in existence in this world in a condition of greater pleasure than pain. The means for the attainment of this end (which all hope for but which none can predict) are left in the hands of the political decision-makers—but with the undisguised hope that the decision-makers will heed the scientists' analyses and not get caught in the grip of dangerous moralisms, utopianisms, etc. It is no wonder that marxist, nationalist, and other ideologies enjoy such power and influence in the world today among statesmen and activists who are looking for meaning, purpose, and direction for political life, In the midst of Western scientific sterility those ideologies are vibrant because they convince decision-makers of what they *ought* to do. Those ideologies give political direction.

Political scientists ought to be bold enough to demand that accurate and progressive scientific work call into question the sterile biases and confining dogmatic assumptions of realists, systems analysts, and functional model builders who stand in the tradition of Enlightenment secularism. They ought to sift carefully through all the work of such scholars, but they ought also to return for a more careful consideration to the works of Plato, the stoics, Augustine, and Aquinas. Indeed, for the sake of authentic political science, they ought to reconsider the vision of the prophets, and of Christ himself, which opens the door to a view of this one world that is altogether more substantial than the Enlightenment hope for world unity through scientific progress. A Christian standpoint, no less than a Platonic or Marxist or contemporary secularistic standpoint, provides a point of departure for the recovery of ancient questions and hypotheses, the investigation of historical realities, and the systematic analysis of contemporary structural identities and functional universalities that mark off the political world of our day. With even greater care and concern for human beings, whom Christians see as created in the image of God, a Christian point of departure can lead political thinkers and students to careful critical reflection on the guiding presuppositions and assumptions that are necessary for the full empirical investigation of political life.

6

Human Rights on a Global Scale?

We have argued that international relations among states ought to be conducted as more than simply a confrontation of powers. The United States should not make its primary objective the goal of keeping itself number one or of seeking its own interests above all else. Individual countries cannot act as if their status in the world can be obtained and maintained single-handedly through acts of sheer military and political will. At the same time, we have argued that principles of international justice and equity ought to be acknowledged and served by the states of this world, including the United States. Could it be, then, that the lively issue of *human rights* is the key to promoting global justice and restraining self-interested power in the contemporary world? Much depends on what is meant by human rights.

The Promise and the Problems

Human rights on a global scale are related to the structure of political and legal authority. The question of rights leads us to ask: which rights? belonging to whom? claimed before what authorities? rooted in what foundation? connected with what responsibilities? A discussion of human rights cannot be abstracted from the real world of states and the obligations of their governments to acknowledge and enforce such rights both domestically and internationally.

The growing recognition of, and demand for, human rights in our time provides evidence that there are universal legal and moral dimensions to politics that cannot be ignored even by the most powerful state. Governments of the world's many states, both separately and jointly, must face the host of obligations that they have for the well-being of their citizens and subjects. In this century, and especially since World War II, hundreds of conferences have been held, declarations signed, and new organizations formed to promote human rights. The best known declaration is probably the United Nations' Universal Declaration of Human Rights, but there are many more.[1] An organization such as Amnesty International works tirelessly to track down evidences of human rights violations all over the world. Pope John Paul II has called the world's attention to the need for greater human rights protection. Former President Jimmy Carter indicated the importance of human rights in some of the first speeches and policies of his administration and Congress has since enacted numerous pieces of legislation that connect American foreign policy with the close observation and promotion of human rights concerns.

Clearly the many conferences, declarations, and organizations seeking to promote recognition and protection of human rights give witness to a process that is motivated by more than each country's narrow concern with its national interest. Many people, including some national and international leaders, recognize that there are norms or standards that should bind and direct the actions of governments both domestically and internationally. Most of the efforts to articulate those norms and to define those standards in international public forums and documents deserve praise, further encouragement, and careful study.[2]

At the same time, however, we must not close our eyes to the fact that there are some serious problems with the way human rights are being conceived, interpreted, and promoted on a global scale today. Moreover, there are many groups and individuals, including government leaders, who believe that a government's concern for human rights should only be expressed and pursued in ways that promote the national interest. William F. Buckley, Jr., for example, believes that there can only be one principal goal of a country's foreign policy, namely, that of "securing the safety of the state . . ."[3] Thus, he recommends that Congress "should repeal existing legislation on the question of human rights . . ." and set up a Commission on Human Rights, entirely separate from the State Department, that would be restricted entirely to reporting factual conditions around the world, with no role in recommending policy.[4]

Buckley and many others are convinced that a global, world-order approach to justice and human rights is foolish, impossible, and self-defeating for sovereign states. A state must be "realistic" in keeping its immediate security interests in mind, and those interests might run directly into conflict with "idealistic" goals of promoting human rights around the globe.

Indeed, a sufficient amount of impractical idealism appears in some of the proposals and documents seeking to promote human rights that one can sense the element of truth in Buckley's argument. If the full protection of human rights on a global scale is conceived as a specific, independent, and unilateral goal of American foreign policy, for example, it will require for its achievement the possibility of being realized according to a certain plan. But the United States cannot single-handedly bring about the full protection of human rights in the world. The whole world is not controlled by the United States. Besides, it, and many of its allies, are conducting other specific policies that do not allow for consideration of human rights protection in other parts of the world. It is foolish indeed to talk about some high moral goal as an ideal while acting in ways that make attaining that goal impossible.[5]

Other difficulties arise as well. Human rights have been

conceived largely as "individual rights" which governments should respect and promote through basic constitutional laws such as the U.S. Bill of Rights. States should grant to individuals freedom of conscience, freedom of speech, freedom from arbitrary arrest and imprisonment, freedom to participate in elections and in government, and so forth. At the same time, since these individual rights are rights within a state, under a government, they have almost always been connected with the goal and ideal that each state should have the right to be free, sovereign, and self-governing. Both individual rights and the rights of states are forms of human rights. The United Nations itself is founded on this principle. But an inherent tension exists between individual rights and the rights of states in the contemporary world.[6]

Without having to study history very carefully, one can easily see that a government's claim to be rightfully independent of any outside interference frequently comes into conflict with outside forces trying to push it toward greater protection of the rights of its individual citizens. The Soviet Union, China, and Cuba are not the only states whose governments have argued that an American Bill of Rights is not in their interest at the present time, or that other states have no right to interfere in their internal affairs. South Korea, Brazil, Iran, and many other countries the United States has supported have said the same thing. Thus, the question must be raised, "Which is the higher principle—a state's autonomy (even if its government violates individual rights) or individual rights, even if others must interfere with a state's independence in order to promote the rights of its citizens?" Who is to judge the quality of various states to decide if the violation of human rights in them merits interference from the outside? Should each state be the judge of all others? Should a state go to war with another state if it believes the second state is violating the rights of its citizens? Does not the act of war itself violate human rights?[7] Could it be that the autonomous sovereignty of states (or the claim of sovereignty) violates human rights by its very nature and structure? Does a framework of universal human rights require, or go hand-in-hand with, a transnational political authority that can protect and advance those rights, much like the fourteenth amendment to the American constitution which gave the federal government authority to protect human rights uniformly in all the sates of the union?

Nor are the difficulties with human rights limited to the fact that "states' rights" and "individual rights" frequently conflict with one another. The fact that the protection of individual rights is not sufficiently strong to secure the rights of groups within states is also a problem. Some groups that think of themselves as separate nations or peoples within existing states, may have no objection to the laws that protect individuals, but they might object to the injustices done to their group as a whole. Indian nations in North America, Quebecois in Canada, Walloon and Flemish peoples in Belgium, the Biafrans in Nigeria are only a few examples of such groups.[8] If, in the name of independence and the *right* of self-determination, such groups seek to separate themselves from the state in which they find themselves, they are almost certain to meet with opposition from the central government which will claim that there is no such thing as the *right* for a group to secede from or undermine the existing state.

Moreover, other types of groups, institutions, and communities within states are not covered or recognized by *individual* rights. Families, schools, churches, different kinds of business enterprises, voluntary organizations, racial groups, political groups, and many others are not necessarily protected by a Bill of Rights for individuals, particularly where the system of political representation operates according to the principle of majority rule.[9] A majority that controls the government, such as in the United States, might rule in a way that protects agreed-upon individual rights, but not recognize the full and proportional rights of some groups, institutions, and communities.

The Challenge Facing Christians

Many efforts to promote human rights today indicate that a world of simple power politics must be rejected. Numerous people and states want a just world that enhances real freedom, opportunity, and protection of rights for all people. But a coherent, worldwide movement leading to global justice by way of the promotion of human rights does not exist. Efforts to promote human rights frequently sound hollow and hypocritical when some states use human rights slogans only to hide their self-interested actions that end up doing little for, and perhaps even hurting human rights in some parts of the world. Many contradictions and inherent tensions exist among different kinds of human rights—the rights of individuals, of groups and institutions, and of states.

It would be a mistake, then, to either jump on an idealistic bandwagon of human rights in the hope that it will lead to global justice, or to reject efforts to promote human rights on a global scale because of cynicism or because of a supposedly realistic argument that such efforts are counter-productive to the national interest. Instead of either uncritical acceptance or skeptical rejection of today's human rights programs, we must come to grips with the real issues that are at stake in order to see what justice requires at an international level.

In the coming decades a tremendous challenge stands before Christians around the world. In the midst of diverse cultures, diverse political systems, and a multitude of deep antagonisms among states and peoples, several universalizing tendencies are struggling with one another.[10] One of those tendencies is technologism and industrialism—the conviction that common techniques and economic progress will eventually harmonize the world. Another is Marxism—the movement that hopes for the eventual fulfillment of global equality and peace after the final destruction of all oppressive economic and political systems. A third tendency is the growth of Christian community in the service of God and neighbor—the power of the Gospel of Jesus Christ building the Kingdom of His Father. If Christians do not work together more vigorously, by the power of the Gospel, to develop sound approaches to public justice, both domestically and globally, then the world will very likely be integrated and unified by other movements which, from a Christian viewpoint, can only do tremendous injustice to individuals, groups, and states.

In the advancement of human rights we should direct our attention to at least three major dimensions in the years ahead.

Who is Man?

The most basic issue at stake in the concern for human rights can be phrased very simply with the question, "Who is Man?" In the mind of some people the most important human right is freedom of individual conscience, freedom to think and speak as one pleases. Some governments, such as the United States, protect that particular individual freedom quite well, but are somewhat less successful in protecting the right of every citizen to have a nutritional diet or to have a job, house, or good education. For others the crucial matter is for governments to provide basic economic well-being for every citizen, even if the social discipline required for such an achievement leaves little room for certain individual freedoms.

The point is simply that one's understanding of human rights will be determined largely by one's view of human nature. Are people primarily individuals, or are they social creatures first? Are they basically and simply animals of a highly advanced character, or is there something more to being human? Are human beings created in the image of God, deserving opportunity, both individually and communally, to unfold their many talents of thought and action, of love and work, of skill and creativity as divine callings?

From a Christian point of view, human beings are neither autonomous individuals nor sovereign builders of states who can create their own rights and fashion their own world. Human beings live beneath God's sovereignty, answerable to His norms of justice, stewardship, and love. Human beings are both individual persons and communal creatures. Citizenship in a state does not exhaust the social responsibility of people, because they are also members of families, schools, businesses, churches, and other communities and institutions. Nor does citizenship in a state provide the highest and final social context in which individuals and groups have responsibility, because the entire earth is God's world and in it all humans share the responsibility of doing justice to their neighbors.

Christians have a tremendous opportunity and responsibility to articulate a biblical view of man that will support a solid program for advancing human rights at all levels of the global community. They have an even greater responsibility to demonstrate their love and concern for neighbors by working for the protection of persons and groups who are now suffering grave injustices. Without a clearly developed view of human nature from a biblical standpoint and a vigorous program of service to oppressed neighbors, Christians will not be able to make a significant contribution to human rights.[11]

The Political Task

The second matter of great importance in the field of human rights is that of clarifying the identity, limits, and task of states as well as the identity, limits, and task of interstate and trans-state organizations. Governments of existing states and international governmental organizations must play a fundamental role in human rights protection. But human rights and responsibilities, seen from the perspective of God's purpose for His people, are more than political and legal rights. The key, then, is to articulate the complex identity of human beings in such a way that the full range of their individual, social, political, and global responsibilities can be identified and protected in public law.

This position means, of course, that human rights are closely tied in with the broader question of the structure of a just state. If the very character of the sovereign state is part of the problem today, then every effort to advance human rights without changing the function and identity of states will lead to failure. If peoples and states around the globe have quite different cultural traditions and are developing in significantly different directions, then perhaps some efforts to promote universal human rights are themselves a cause of serious injustice, since they might manifest an imposition of one tradition's ideas and designs on the whole world. Human rights are tied in with the very meaning of justice and injustice in states and thus cannot be protected or enhanced in abstraction from actual state and interstate structures.[12]

Some of the hyprocrisy and inconsistency of current human rights programs are due to the fact that states frequently use those programs as tools of their short-range, self-interested foreign policies. Sometimes the United States finds it advantageous to call loudly for human rights for Russian dissidents; at other times it decides that it has no interest at all in calling for human rights for political prisoners in Guatemala or South Korea. It is clear, then, that a discussion of human rights cannot get far without evaluating the justice and injustice of broader foreign policies.

If human rights derive from transcendent norms of justice that cannot be manipulated by states as tools of their foreign policies, then a comprehensive picture of global justice must be articulated as a normative responsibility that obligates states. The difficulty of achieving such a comprehensive articulation and of getting states to submit themselves to those norms must then be taken into account in designing both slogans and programs for human rights protection. Neither idealistic optimism nor cynical pessimism should grow out of the desire to articulate and obey the normative responsibility that states have for domestic and international justice.

Resolution of Conflicts

Finally, in the coming decades serious attention must be given to resolving the conflicts that are evident among individual rights, group rights, state rights, and global justice. Do people have a *right* to enjoy a just government, or are human rights simply rights that individuals hold over and against governments? If states and peoples are growing increasingly interdependent, does that call for the growth of *supranational* government authorities similar to the early historical development of the United States federal government or the emergence of the European Economic Community after World War II? If centralized states, as presently organized, fail to do justice to some peoples and groups within them, such as the Kurds in Iran, the Basques in Spain, and many peoples in the Soviet Union, should the emphasis fall on *decentralization* of political authority in the years ahead? Or should the growth of supranational authorities and the decentralization of power go hand-in-hand?[13]

While it is essential for governments to move away from arbitrary arrests and punishment, away from dictatorial rule through torture and terror, and toward fair and just rule by law under which citizens have rights of free assembly, speech, conscience, and promise of due process of law, it is also the case that the years ahead will find more and more states preoccupied with basic needs of food, water, health care, shelter, and clothing. Given the population explosion and increasing competition for the available food and water on earth, many people do not have the luxury to be concerned about more sophisticated rights while they suffer malnutrition and even starvation.

Here is an explosive global condition that comes back to the conflicts that exist among people, their various associations, and different levels of government. Do the wealthy countries of the northern hemisphere have a *right* to retain their wealth and power while other states cannot manage to feed their people? Do states have the *right* to spend billions of dollars for weapons of war to "protect" themselves while millions of unprotected citizens are starving?

The United States is in a position where it can help to make a significant contribution to the resolution of some of these problems if it chooses to do so. It has wealth and power; it has a federal structure of government with many levels of government authority; it has a strong tradition of concern for individual rights. If Americans, especially those who are Christians, can rise above selfish preoccupation with their own wealth and power to go beyond a focus on individual rights to a broader conception of group rights, and give more attention to the complex issue of human rights on a global scale, then much can be accomplished in cooperation with other states and peoples both within each state and among them all at the international level.

7

International Justice:
Is It Possible?

Survival with some sort of autonomy, peace, prosperity, and dignity is increasingly the concern of the weakest as well as the most powerful modern states today. Most states, however, are becoming aware of the emptiness of the slogan, "the right to self-determination." Whether it is the problem of a single-product trading market for a small country or the problem of heavy dependence on Middle East oil for industrial Europe, or the problem of multinational corporations controlling national politics, every modern state is increasingly confronted with the fact of international *interdependence* throughout this *one* world.

In the context of such growing interdependence, *international justice* should be the dominant concern of states today; it should be acknowledged as the true norm that transcends and brings to judgment all other motives and "principles" that have guided nations in their relationship with each other. Without justice there will be no peace and security based simply on national self-determination, independence, balance of power, national self-interest, stability, maintenance of the status quo, or industrial development.

If we look carefully at the historical development of international relations, we discover that the rules, powers, and motives that have directed the relations among nations to this very day have frequently led precisely to critical situations of *injustice* which then explode and demolish the stability, independence, balance, interests, and development of states.

The Historical Context of Contemporary International Relations

The present character of global international relations, we must remember, has been determined largely by the rise of an aggressive and secularized West. The political, economic, and technical powers of the West have guided Western expansion and Western imperialism-colonialism as well as twentieth-century global integration. Moreover, Western ideas of revolution, independence, national self-determination, and free relations among sovereign states are the ideas and dreams that have led to modern mass nationalism, anti-colonial revolutions, and international organizations based on the primary principle of national sovereignty. Using the title and thesis of C.B. Macpherson's book on English political theory from Hobbes to Locke,[1] we might say that the "possessive individualism" of Western liberalism has now become the dominant motive of global international relations. In the international arena, possessive individualism usually goes by the name of "national self-interest." And the same problems that have made "possessive individualistic liberalism" inadequate as a principle for rendering public justice *within* modern democratic states make it inadequate for establishing just relations *among* "possessive self-interested nations." What are some of these problems in a global community dominated by Western influence? Is it possible that international justice can overcome those problems?

The medieval European empire of Christendom, from which the modern European states emerged, generally acknowledged God's sovereignty expressed through natural and revealed law as interpreted chiefly by the Church. With the gradual breakdown of an integrated Christendom, men like Hugo Grotius and nations like Britain, Holland, France, and Spain turned to look for universal "natural" principles that would not be dependent upon ecclesiastical or supranaturally revealed authority. Grotius, who is usually considered to be the father of modern international law, was convinced that he had discovered a few formal principles, of a rational, natural, legal character, that he thought would guarantee peace if nations would freely submit to them. For example, he argued that a nation ought to make restitution for any harm done to another and that signed agreements or treaties ought to be kept *(pacta sunt servanda)*.

The problem with Grotius' principles, however, is that they say little or nothing about the justice or injustice of actual circumstances and conditions in which states find themselves at any point in history. What about the unequal distribution of the world's natural resources? What about the technical developments that give one state a military superiority over others? What about the superiority of one state over another at the time that a treaty between them is signed? What about population differences, natural disasters, or a host of other historical factors that affect relations among nations? Within the bounds of "natural law" as Grotius interpreted it, a nation could freely seek its own self-interest in an entirely legal way that might nevertheless perpetuate international injustice to the breaking point. In fact, we have today, in the growing economic power of some countries and the growing poverty of others, an example of precisely this point. Possessive, individualistic, self-seeking nationalism has not provided a basis for international justice among interdependent nations even within the framework of international law.

The historical process of Western nationalism leading to imperialistic colonialism, followed by worldwide, anti-colonial revolutions that aim for national self-determination, has offered far too little insight into the tasks their governments ought to pursue in order to establish justice both domestically and internationally. Many Americans believe that the maintenance of their preeminence in the world is both economically and militarily in national self-interest and is also essential for world peace and stability. Latin Americans can argue with equal force, however, that such preeminence on the part of the United States is not in *their* interest and will eventually lead to greater instability in the world as smaller nations are forced to seize power in order to compete with America.

All forms of self-determining nationalism, therefore, are threatened by every limit to the desired self-sufficiency, and so nations must act in every way possible to overcome those limits, which then means an aggressive imperialism. The Argentinian Mariano Grondona, states boldly that the "new world" in which we live today "is a world in which each nation, large or small, is bent on obtaining the greatest advantage for itself. National interest stands first in the scale of values."[2]

Our world today, increasingly in need of international justice among interdependent nations, finds itself caught in the tight web of a secularized Western influence that has led independent states to try, for four centuries, to build a secular world community on the basis of nationalistic, individualistic, possessive self-interest. The answer to the world's present need for international justice will not be found in the continuation of this trend through pragmatic power politics, no matter if that power is directed by the West toward maintenance of the status quo, or by nonwestern states toward revolutionary nationalism.

International Law

The hope of scholars such as Grotius was that some kind of international legal order might be established that would guide "enlightened" nations away from war and self-destruction to the point where various peaceful means could be used to settle disputes, arbitrate conflicts, and keep the peace. Historically, however, the development of modern international law has been controlled almost from the beginning by "positivism," that is, by the conviction that law should be built up on the basis of the practice of states in their actual conduct of international relations rather than by "pure natural reason." As a matter of fact, international relations have been conducted with this assumption by independent sovereign states yielding the consequence that the most powerful ones have been the chief authors of international law. International law, in other words, has not been the product of a principled effort among all states to discern the requirements of global justice, but a product of the pragmatic relations of the most powerful nations and blocs of nations. Treaties, when signed, may well be kept for a time, but usually the treaty reflects the best interests of the stronger signatory or signatories rather than the interests of the weaker. Equally powerful states might establish a temporary peace through a treaty or international organization that balances their power, but such a treaty is no guarantee of world justice, nor, generally speaking, can the weaker states challenge impositions by the stronger.

The concern for world peace today emerges consistently from this positivistic, pragmatic framework. Thus, world peace is not really the first priority of most states. Treaties and international agreements that concern the United States in her relations with the Soviet Union, China, Europe, and Latin America are designed with the hope of advancing American interests or of maintaining the status quo. Richard R. Fagan argues, for instance, that recent American relations with Chile have *not* reflected a more congenial concern for the interests of the world's weaker states. North American states continue their attempts to manage the globe through moderating their own "big power" conflicts.

As a corollary, this vision "accepts as inevitable the persistence of large-scale misery and repression. It enables the disfavored *many* to be kept under control by the favored *few*." Its basic amorality derives from the expendability of any and all experiments and people who threaten the new world order now being assembled. As such, it is deeply committed to the perpetuation of the status quo, albeit a status quo which now fully accepts and integrates the U.S.S.R. and mainland China.

The struggle is thus recast in terms of the developed (or powerful) against the less developed (or less powerful), with the latter the subject of malevolent attention whenever interests clash or experimentation seems to be running unchecked in directions that include greater national autonomy.[3]

Not only do the weakest states stand in a dangerous and often helpless position, but the only avenue that appears to be open for their influence in the future is that of gaining sufficient power through whatever means possible in order to play the self-interest power game—itself a dangerous and often lethal option. Obviously the tensions and instabilities resulting from such a game are a threat to all states but particularly to those that hold the greatest power and influence. Thus it continues to be in the interest of the strongest nations, or so it apears to them, to fashion international law in a way that will not greatly alter the status quo until a great new accumulation of power threatens to blow it apart.

The question to raise here is not whether international law will ever be "purified" after it has been so thoroughly stamped by political "power." It can only and should only be a political law for political powers. The real question concerns the proper *norm* for international law: "Will international law be made to serve the cause of international justice, or will it be directed primarily toward the ends of national self-interest promoted by the most powerful states?" If our positivistic age is beyond the point where a supposedly universal, rational, natural law has any significance for shaping international law, it is also apparently far removed from the only true Lawgiver who can open the eyes of nations to their true responsibility for one another. But this distance from the world's true King does not undermine the validity of Christ's Lordship and of His justice. Precisely in the midst of the crying injustice that surrounds us, we may be able to see quite clearly what the law among nations *ought to be* as it calls our international corruption into question and up for judgment.

Some Dominant Motives of Today's Global Relations

The dominant principle or motive that seems to control world politics today is, as we have seen, the desire for national sovereignty, national independence, or national self-determined preeminence. It is not surprising that colonial territories and nations challenged their colonial masters by making use of the very principles of freedom, independence, and democracy which those masters had claimed and proclaimed. Anti-colonialism is today an almost universal, self-evident truth having the character of a "higher law."

What is seldom emphasized, however, is that the right of self-determination provides no guidance for the promotion of national or international justice except insofar as it stands against imperialism or colonialism; even then it often functions in an ambiguous or contradictory fashion. Rupert Emerson exposes the problem this way: the United Nations Declaration on Granting Independence (1960), after asserting that all people have the right of self-determination, goes on to impose sharp limits on that right: "Any attempt aimed at the partial or total disruption of the national unity and territorial integrity of a country is incompatible with the purposes and principles of the Charter of the United Nations."

Emerson then comments:

> As the imperial power could not acknowledge the right of its dependencies to overthrow the existing colonial govern-

117

ments of their own free will by revolutionary action, so the newly established states cannot tolerate having their rule challenged by disaffected minorities or regions, no matter how good the claim of the latter to separate national existence may be. *My* right to self-determination against those who oppress me is obviously unimpeachable, but *your* claim to exercise such a right against me is wholly inadmissible.[4]

If Belgium in the early nineteenth century was justified in leaving the Kingdom of the Netherlands, then what is wrong with the Flemish and Walloon "nations" going their separate ways today? If Canada has some right to be independent of Britain, then why should not Quebec be independent of Canada? If the United States was justified in its original revolt, then what was so improper in the revolt of the Confederate states against the union? If black African nations are justified in carrying through independence movements, then why should not the Indians of North America and Latin America be free from white domination?

The point is that the cry for nationalistic sovereignty cannot clearly define the boundaries of a state much less the task of a state. Whatever the justice of anti-colonialism and anti-imperialism, these movements will have to be fashioned by a broader motive of domestic and international justice if any good is to come of them. If, for example, the contemporary, Western Pax Americana ought to be ended, even as the Pax Britannica and the Pax Romana came to an end, then a positive conception of the just interrelation of free states must be unfolded to displace the merely negative reaction *against* imperialism and colonialism. The mere emergence and growth of independent states gives little guidance toward the development of equitable relations among them.

A second dominant motive of global relations among states today is also rooted in Western power and mythology. It is the conviction that economic growth as measured by Western industrial standards is a primary and necessary national priority. But again we find that this goal or motive in itself provides little help in establishing justice either domestically or internationally.

The United States is happy to have the opportunity to invest in Latin America, which may or may not be much help to Latin American economic development, but only so long as such investments aid their own economic development and political power. Many Latin American states are anxious to receive capital, but only if strings are not attached in a way that will allow the United States' continued dominance economically, or in a way that will require a radical change in the domestic dominance of wealthy classes over poorer classes in the Latin American countries. Economic growth appears to be a necessity politically, yet it is not clear how it can occur with any international justice when the sole or primary criterion for judging it is national economic progress as defined by the states.

It is not at all strange that the oil-producing countries have organized as a power bloc against the oil-importing countries for their own economic advantage. It is not a bit surprising that countries in Latin America and elsewhere have been expropriating foreign-owned industries in order to control them for their own economic advancement. The wealthy nations are beginning to cry out against the injustice of it all, but their cry is mocked by those whose cries went unheard for so long and who learned how to wield such power by watching the practice of the now whimpering giants.

If the West has convinced the world that industrial growth, like independence and self-determination, is one of the chief goals of national life, then should we be surprised that new injustices (some of them now perpetrated against the West) will occur as new nations struggle frantically to attain their own independent prosperity? Dare we feign indignation when we discover that other nations are no more interested in justice for us than we have been interested in justice for them?

Today other voices argue that the primary motive or rule that should structure relationships in the global village is the avoidance of nuclear war. The argument sounds rather like that of the philosopher Thomas Hobbes when he sought to establish the very existence of a commonwealth on the basis of the fear that each man had of his neighbor because of the war of all against all. Nations, like individuals, the argument goes, cannot even continue to argue and debate and fight and struggle with one another if they don't maintain their existence, so the preservation of existing states from nuclear destruction ought to be the ultimate controlling concern in international relations today.

Such an argument has some plausibility, of course, but it is not sufficient when it comes to the question of *why* states should continue existing, or the question of *what else* existing states ought to do in addition to guarding against a nuclear holocaust. Even if the nations of the world are able to keep from using nuclear weapons on a massive scale for the next few hundred years, that will not do justice to the billions of people who continue to starve; it will not resolve the injustice of a few nations continuing to expand at the expense of the many; it will not guarantee that nuclear blackmail will not become the dominant game in international politics.

It is not at all clear that the world is in a safer condition today after the signing of the Nuclear Non-Proliferation Treaty and after the United States and the Soviet Union have negotiated some arms limitations agreements. The easing of cold war tensions for a period of time may give some sense of relief, and the longer we live *with* nuclear weapons *without* using them may give us the sense of stability that an established tradition provides. But nuclear weapons are still controlled by the same powers that control conventional weapons, and we know how the latter have been employed since World War II in Eastern Europe, Southeast Asia, South Asia, Latin America, Africa, the Middle East, Cyprus and elsewhere.

No equitable, long-term resolution of problems relating

to nuclear weapons is possible without the resolution of more fundamental international conflicts and injustices. SALT talks can be carried on decade after decade, but as long as the participants in such discussions are powerful self-seeking states assuming some sort of national self-interest as the chief aim of their foreign policies, there will be no reprieve from Hobbesian fear on all sides. Harmony and justice cannot grow out of the seedbed of fear. One day in the future a world-dominant Leviathan may prove to be the only pragmatic answer available for dealing with nuclear power for nations that have failed to seek justice when they were able to do so. Nuclear war must be avoided; the arms race will bring no security; but it is not enough to make the chief aim of international relations the avoidance of nuclear war. That is a false abstraction.

American Foreign Policy

Most commentators agree that the modern state is im-mensely strong, all-encompassing, and quite unprepared to wither away. Jacques Ellul contends:

> Governmental action is applied to a constantly growing number of realms. The means through which the state can act are constantly growing. Its personnel and its functions are constantly growing. Its responsibilities are growing. All this goes hand in hand with inevitable centralization and with the total organization of society in the hands of the state. The nation-state is the most important reality in our day.[5]

If the nation-state is the central seat of world power to-day, then consider the implications for international politics in view of the fact that the United States is still the single most powerful state. Since American foreign policy has been con-ducted with a view to what is in its national interest, and the interests of the American people have had much to do with industrial growth and ever-increasing consumption, it is not hard to understand the government's attitude toward the conduct of foreign policy. American life, which has become defined more and more by economic factors in the twentieth century, has been undergoing a "politization" process in the direction of a one-dimensional society that does not bode well for international justice. The national interest for which American foreign policy is conducted supposedly exhausts the totality of interests and concerns that Americans have, and purportedly represents the complete understanding they have of their nation's tasks and responsibilities in the world.

President Nixon was convinced that one of our chief aims was to become self-sufficient in energy by 1980 so that we could continue living without interruption as the world's preeminent economy. President Ford announced to the Congress in January, 1975 that the state of the Union was not good, meaning that prosperity and economic growth were not what they used to be. By 1980 the United States was neither self-sufficient in energy nor able to resolve growing difficulties in its economy, as President Carter made abundantly clear on numerous occasions. The problem with these presidential views is that they make it impossible for us to see the great variety of human needs with which governmental justice ought to be concerned, both within the United States and around the world. Governments in the developed world are responsible for more than simply national economic growth, and even on that level, nations around the world, and some people within the wealthy countries, are being harmed by national growth patterns in the West.

What is required at this point in history is a massive fight against a narrow, economically-qualified political process that is leading the American government (and many other governments) farther and farther away from a concern for multifaceted social justice at home and abroad.

The "totalitarian state" need not be limited to communist or fascist forms. It may take the form of a democratic state where the people have become preoccupied with a single political-economic dimension of life and where they serve the state as the sole lord of life and prosperity. If the fight against the reductionistic politization process is not fought, then every kind of domestic and international injustice will continue to be perpetrated under the banner of American and other "national interests."

The fact that some countries consider American foreign aid policy to be selfish is not understood by most Americans precisely because we have been taught to assume that any assistance the United States gives in the process of its legitimate self-seeking efforts is true generosity; consequently, we are convinced that we have been overly generous throughout our history. American education is not designed to call into question the whole principle of "America first," but is programmed to show students how generous the United States has been and how ungrateful many recipients of aid have been. Foreigners, in other words, ought to be thankful for whatever they get rather than complain about what they don't get, since the American government is not a charity organization and it owes nothing to anyone but its own. Former Secretary of State Henry Kissinger expressed this attitude in a speech in Los Angeles in 1975.

> The Administration is convinced that foreign aid to be viable must serve American national interests above all, including the broad interest we have in a stable world. If an important American interest is served by the aid relationship, it is a wise investment; if not, our resources are being squandered, even if we have no specific grievances against the recipient.

With respect to another key problem—the "interventionist" tactics of powerful governments like the United States in areas such as Latin-America—Richard Fagan argues:

> There is no reason to believe that the U.S. posture toward Chile and the array of hostile actions taken constitute an

exceptional case, something we shall not see again. As long as the United States continues to evaluate the poorer and weaker countries of the world in terms of what each can contribute to the grand design—or the real and imagined threats that each poses to that grand design—there can be no assurances of nonintervention. In some place, at some time, some government or movement short on power but long on alternative visions of development will surely be questing after social justice at home, and more autonomy and a fairer shake in its international dealings. And as long as such quests tend to get defined as inimical to the national interests of the United States, the economic and political pressures against the recalcitrant government will mount, the CIA will sally forth from Langley, and eventually the deception and manipulation will touch the halls of Congress and the American people.

Oversight committees, citations for contempt, vigorous and watchful news media, and less secrecy in government may ameliorate the situation, but they will not end it. The root problems lie in the definitions of the national interest that are used and the policies that are based on them.[6]

One of the problems with the definition of national interest now being employed by the United States is its pragmatism and ambiguity. The U.S. State Department, in working with other executive departments in the service of the President, does not have sole authority in shaping foreign policy, nor does it work with a publicly agreed upon, principled conception of international justice as the unifying theme and norm of its programs. The often contradictory influences of competing interest groups within the United States are nearly always manifest in the shaping of foreign policy just as they are in the shaping of domestic policy. The influence of labor, or agriculture, or big business, or any number of other special interests will be felt in different ways at different times. And each of these interests functions in its own possessive, individualistic way as something of a microcosm of the nation as a whole in its international relations.

The only way to conduct foreign policy in such a context is for the President, Secretary of State, Secretary of Defense, and other leading officials to work from day to day in a pragmatic, give-and-take manner. This resort to pragmatism explains why the negotiated "peace" settlement in Vietnam has not led to peace, and why, after "Good Neighbor Policies" and "Alliances for Progress" and countless other programs, the United States is still not trusted as a friend by the other nations. Not only is it difficult to discern at any given time what American foreign policy is, but often a contradictory or radically different policy appears later. Instead of attempting to institutionalize basic principles of international justice through close cooperation with other states, most countries work from day to day in a positivistic, pragmatic way to see what advantages can be gained for themselves.

Pragmatism thus seems to be a very willing servant of the nationalistic, self-interested motives that we have already discussed. It allows a nation to put off any challenge to work for justice as too idealistic or unrealistic rather than face up to its own *unjust* policies. It allows government officials to play on the fears of citizens—fears of communism, or depression, or losing national prestige—in order to try to gain some momentary advantage in dealing with other nations. It allows grave injustices to be covered up as mistakes or "miscalculations" due to not having all the facts at the time a decision was made. But pragmatism also produces victims by the score both outside and inside the country—dying victims of the Vietnam "peace"; poverty stricken victims of inflation; starving victims of international food conferences; political victims of American "aid" to Chile, Iran, Israel, and Korea.

The ongoing pragmatic search for America's national self-interest may appear to many to be succeeding in keeping us number one, but only those blinded by nationalistic selfishness can fail to see that the resulting lack of international justice leads to turmoil, instability, and further injustice in the world.

What Must Be Done?

Is international justice possible? The question may sound like a pragmatic one, given the use of the word "possible." And if it is asked that way, the best answer would seem to be Kissinger's when he once remarked that the contemporary issues of international politics,

> have little to do with the age-old tension between morality and expediency. Foreign policy, by its nature, must combine a desire to achieve the ideal with a recognition of what is practical. The fact of sovereignty implies compromise and each compromise involves an element of pragmatism. On the other hand, a purely expedient policy will lack roots and become the prisoner of events. The difficult choices are not between principle and expediency but between two objectives both of which are good, or between courses of action both of which are difficult or dangerous. To achieve a fruitful balance is the central dilemma of foreign policy.[7]

This response grants priority to national "sovereignty" as a pure and permanent fact that implies that any conception of transnationalistic justice is an unreachable ideal. Kissinger furthermore establishes the *principle* of pragmatic, competitive compromise in a way that simply obliterates the possibility of any factual evaluation from the viewpoint of "justice" or "morality." The fact that he wants to reject a rootless expediency only means that his pragmatic decisions will reflect the "national interest" and will consistently acknowledge the necessity of compromise in doing what is practical in any given situation. It is difficult, however, to distinguish this kind of pragmatism from expediency.

If, however, we ask whether or not international justice is possible from a principled non-pragmatic standpoint, we can be concerned legitimately with what *ought* to be the case in international relations whether or not that is "possible" within the framework of the "fact of sovereignty." The answer to such a question would then help to clarify the kinds of norms that can serve for the critical evaluation of unjust situations and would enable those who live through countless future injustices to understand the truth of what is happening. Such an answer might also provide help and encouragement to those in political office who *do* want to adopt a new perspective or framework for international policy decisions.

● *International justice will be possible* to the extent that international relations begin to reflect a withering away of ''national self-interest'' as their primary norm and motive. This is not to say that states must begin denying their perceived interests or serving only other nations' interests. Rather, the whole possessive individualistic framework of self-centered nationalism must be overcome by states beginning to serve their own citizens *and, cooperatively*, the citizens of other states by means of true justice. The national interest, in other words, must give way to, or be redefined as, *the interest of justice for all people* rather than remain the pragmatic tool of governments seeking prosperity or power for one group of people or one nation at the expense of other peoples or nations.

The ready reply that such a thing will never happen, given modern nationalism and human selfishness in general, can only have the value of warning us that the world's doom is certain. Those who believe that the pragmatic response of ''It isn't possible'' can itself serve as a norm for realistic action are only fooling themselves.

● *International justice will also become possible* to the extent that the historical development of contemporary international injustice (for example, the extreme wealth of some countries coupled with the extreme poverty of others) is understood in all of its details and dealt with gradually and responsibly by all nations, *beginning with the self-critical change of those nations that enjoy the present advantages*. The wealthy and powerful nations of the world must not be allowed to interpret history as an accident, or as the survival of the fittest, or as the fruit of their responsibility coupled with the irresponsibility of other peoples and nations, or as the blessing of God on the wealthy and powerful coupled with His condemnation of the poor and the weak.

The United States and other major states must become increasingly willing to take responsible, definite, and careful steps in the direction of justice for all states. The demand is not for the United States or the Soviet Union or Japan or West Germany to throw down its power to become a charity organization, but to begin consistently, faithfully, and steadily to act in a way that will encourage the cooperative effort of more and more nations to seek true justice for all people. Some of the implications of such a movement should be superficially obvious to anyone who knows anything about the wealth and power of Europe, North America, Japan, and the Soviet Union in the world today. The details of such a movement should not and could not be worked out in blind or naive ignorance of the fact that most of the world's nations have already learned to play the game by the old rules and might not be willing immediately to trust the powerful nations of the world in their new venture.

● *International justice will become possible* to the extent that "development" as defined by Western consumption and industrial expansion is rejected. If development can be enlarged, unfolded, and reconceived to capture the true breadth and diversity of human life on earth involving all of the creative energies, social interrelationships, and cultural complexities of our humanness, then it will be possible for governments cooperatively to reduce the overconsumption of food and resources by the few in order that the many may be able not only to eat but also to think, speak, write, paint, sing, weave, build, and travel.

● *International justice is possible* to the extent that states begin to work cooperatively toward true freedom and interdependent diversity rather than continuing along the road toward competitive independence and self-determination. "Independence" and "self-determination" are slogans belonging to a Western humanistic myth. That myth can only mean that the poorer and less powerful nations will be manipulated by the wealthy and powerful ones until they get strong or wealthy enough to do some manipulating of their own. Moreover, not even the wealthy and powerful nations are truly independent of one another. The true freedom that is necessary for a plurality of states will be gained only through cooperation based on a just and equitable conception of interdependence. The alternative to true justice is not competitive self-sufficiency but eventually a totalitarian world state, the Hobbesian Leviathan, the rule of anti-Christ.

● *International justice will be possible* to the extent that Western humanistic conceptions of international law (whether rationalistic, positivistic, nationalistic, or any combination of these) are replaced by the biblical, neighbor-serving practice of justice, as will happen, in any event when all things are set in order through the culminating revelation of Jesus Christ. Even at this moment, states are called to, and held responsible for, the exercise of the authority granted to them by the earth's only true King. Failure to exercise that authority for international justice will only incur God's wrath, whereas steps in the direction of biblically informed justice can mean, even now, the anticipatory peace of God's Kingdom.

Notes to Chapter 1

1. For an understanding of the Old Middle Kingdom and its view of the world, see John Patton Davies, Jr., *Dragon by the Tail* (New York: W.W. Norton & Co., 1972), pp. 9-56; Barbara W. Tuchman, *Stilwell and the American Experience in China 1911-45* (New York: Bantam Books, 1971), pp. 30-51; O. Edmund Clubb, *China and Russia: The "Great Game"* (New York: Columbia University Press, 1971), pp. 1-29; and Eric Voegelin, *The Ecumenic Age*, vol. 4 of *Order and History* (Baton Rouge: Louisiana State University Press, 1974), Chap. 6, "The Chinese Ecumene," pp. 272-299.
2. On the Roman imperial idea of world order, see Mario A. Levi, *Political Power in the Ancient World*, translated by Jane Costello (New York: Mentor Books, 1965), pp. 149-217; and Walter Ullmann, *Medieval Political Thought* (Baltimore: Penguin Books, 1965), pp. 11-37.
3. On the medieval Holy Roman Empire, see Ullmann, *Medieval Political Thought*, pp. 38-129; and Denys Hay, *Europe: The Emergence of an Idea* (New York: Harper Torchbooks, 1957), pp. 16-55.
4. See F. Parkinson, *The Philosophy of International Relations* (Beverly Hills: Sage Publications, 1977), pp. 27-60; Ernst Cassirer, *The Myth of the State* (New Haven: Yale University Press, 1946), pp. 116-162.
5. See the excellent analysis of western society by Bob Goudzwaard, *Capitalism and Progress: A Diagnosis of Western Society*, translated by Josina Van Nuis Zylstra (Toronto: Wedge Publishing Foundation; and Grand Rapids: Eerdmans Publishing Co., 1979).
6. Alexander Solzhenitsyn has written a challenging essay that raises many questions about this issue: "Repentance and Self-Limitation in the Life of Nations," in Solzhenitsyn, et al.,

From Under the Rubble (Boston: Little, Brown & Co.), pp. 105-143.

7. With special attention focused on Europe, Stanley Hoffman provides some helpful insights into this problem in his essay, "Obstinate or Obsolete? The Fate of the Nation-State and the Case of Western Europe," in Morton A. Kaplan, ed., *Great Issues of International Politics* (Chicago: Aldine Publishing Co., 1970), pp. 85-122.

8. There has been a limited effort at cooperation among European Christian Democrats and groups in other parts of the world who associate with that tradition. A publication from one recent seminar held in The Hague on the occasion of the one hundredth anniversary of the Dutch Antirevolutionary Party is *Christian Political Options* (The Hague: Dr. A. Kuyperstichting, 1979). This volume brings together essays and addresses of Christian Democrats from various parts of the world.

Notes to Chapter 2

1. Stephen E. Ambrose, *Rise to Globalism: American Foreign Policy, 1938-1976*, revised edition (New York: Penguin Books, 1976), p. 11.

2. Consider the following examples of recent interpretations: Ambrose, *Rise to Globalism* (noted above); Richard J. Barnet, *Roots of War* (New York: Atheneum, 1972); Franz Schurmann, *The Logic of World Power* (New York: Pantheon Books, 1974); Robert C. Johansen, *The National Interest and the Human Interest* (Princeton: Princeton University Press, 1980); George Grant, *Technology and Empire* (Toronto: House of Anansi, 1969), pp. 15-40, 63-78; and Bernard Zylstra, "Modernity and the American Empire," *International Reformed Bulletin*, First and Second Quarter (1977), pp. 3-19.

3. Helpful discussions of nuclear weapons, nuclear strategy, and the SALT talks can be found in David Ziegler, *War, Peace, and International Politics* (Boston: Little, Brown, and Co., 1977), pp. 64-83, 215-241; John Herz, *The Nation-State and the Crisis of World Politics* (New York: David McKay, 1976); and Robert Johansen, *The National Interest and the Human Interest*, pp. 38-125.

4. Barnet, *Roots of War*, p. 24.
5. Grant, *Technology and Empire*, pp. 26-27.
6. *Ibid.*, p. 27. Compare the contrasting perspectives on technology of Egbert Schuurman, *Reflections on the Technological Society* (Toronto: Wedge Publishing Foundation, 1977), and Daniel J. Boorstin, *The Republic of Technology* (New York: Harper Colophon Books, 1978).
7. Barnet, *Roots of War*, p. 33.
8. *Ibid.*, pp. 74-75.
9. On the identity, problems, needs, and expectations of the Third World, see Gunnar Myrdal, *The Challenge of World Poverty* (New York: Pantheon Books, 1970); Myrdal and Seth S. King, *Asian Drama: An Inquiry into the Poverty of Nations* (New York: Vintage Books, 1971); Enrique Dussel, *History and the Theology of Liberation*, translated by John Drury (Maryknoll, N.Y.: Orbis Books, 1976); Robert C. Johansen, *The National Interest and the Human Interest*, pp. 126-363; Thierry de Montbrial, "For a New World Economic Order," and Tom J. Farer, "The United States and the Third World: A Basis for Accommodation," in *Foreign Affairs* (October, 1975), pp. 61-97.
10. Ambrose, *Rise to Globalism*, p. 19.
11. Barnet, *Roots of War*, pp. 197-198. See Barnet and R. Müller, *Global Reach: The Power of the Multinational Corporations* (New York: Simon and Schuster, 1974); and Harry Antonides, *Multinationals and the Peaceable Kingdom* (Toronto: Clarke, Irwin, and Co., 1978).
12. Goudzwaard, *A Christian Political Option* (Toronto: Wedge Publishing Foundation, 1972), p. 18.
13. Barnet, *Roots of War*, p. 120.

Notes to Chapter 3

1. Niebuhr, *Moral Man and Immoral Society*, originally published in 1932 by Charles Scribner's Sons, New York. For further discussion of this realism/idealism debate, see: Robert De Vries "Moral Principle and Foreign Policy-Making," *Christian Scholar's Review*, vol. VI, no. 4 (1977), pp. 303-316; John Herz, *Political Realism and Political Idealism* (Chicago:

University of Chicago Press, 1951); Thomas I. Cook and Malcolm Moos, *Power Through Purpose: The Realism of Idealism as a Basis for Foreign Policy* (Baltimore: The Johns Hopkins Press, 1954); and James E. Dougherty and Robert L. Pfaltzgraff, Jr., *Contending Theories of International Relations* (Philadelphia: J.B. Lippincott, 1971).

2. See the discussion of these different figures in Kenneth N. Waltz, *Man, the State, and War: A Theoretical Analysis* (New York: Columbia University Press, 1954, 1959), pp. 20-41, 103-123, 145-158. See also Reinhold Niebuhr, *Christianity and Power Politics* (New York: Scribner's, 1940), and *Christian Realism and Political Problems* (New York: Scribner's, 1953); Edward H. Buehrig, *Woodrow Wilson and the Balance of Power* (Bloomington: Indiana University Press, 1955); John Hobson, *Towards International Government* (London: George Allen and Unwin, 1951).

3. Henry A. Kissinger, *A World Restored: The Politics of Conservatism in a Revolutionary Age* (New York: Grosset and Dunlap, 1964).

4. *Ibid.*, p. 172, quoted in James E. Dornan, Jr. and Diane S. Dornan, "The Works of Henry A. Kissinger," *The Political Science Reviewer*, vol. V (Fall, 1975), pp. 53-54.

5. Quoted in Dornan and Dornan, "The Works of Henry Kissinger," p. 54.

6. *Ibid.*, p. 116.

7. *Ibid.*, p. 121.

8. *Ibid.*

9. *Ibid.*, p. 122.

10. See, for example, Richard N. Cooper, ed., *A Reordered World: Emerging Economic Problems* (Washington, D.C.: Potomac Associates with Foreign Policy, 1973).

11. Pinder, "Economic Diplomacy," in *World Politics*, edited by James N. Rosenau, Kenneth W. Thompson, and Gavin Boyd (New York: The Free Press, 1976), p. 316.

12. *Ibid.*

13. *Ibid.*, p. 317.

14. One example of some important thinking that should be studied and criticized from an integrally Christian standpoint is a collection of essays edited by Saul H. Mendlovitz, *On the Creation of a Just World Order: Preferred Worlds for the*

1990's (New York: The Free Press, 1975). A very helpful start for Christians, particularly in the economic sphere, can be found in: Bob Goudzwaard's *Aid for the Overdeveloped West* (Toronto: Wedge Publishing Foundation, 1975); E.F. Schumacher, *Small is Beautiful: Economics as if People Mattered* (New York: Harper and Row Perennial Library, 1973); Gunner Myrdal, *The Challenge of World Poverty* (New York: Random House Pantheon Books, 1970); Ronald J. Sider, *Rich Christians in an Age of Hunger: A Biblical Study* (Downers Grove, Ill.: Intervarsity Press, 1977).

15. Johan Galtung, "International Relations and International Conflicts: A Sociological Approach," and "East-West Interaction Patterns," both cited in Marshall R. Singer, "The Foreign Policies of Small developing States," *World Politics*, edited by Rosenau, Thompson, and Boyd, p. 271 ff.
16. Singer, *Ibid.*, pp. 271-272.
17. *Ibid.*, p. 273.
18. *Ibid.*, p. 282.
19. For greater detail and evaluation of United States-Chile relations during this period, see Robert C. Johansen, *The National Interest and the Human Interest*, Chap. 4, "The United States and Human Rights in Chile," pp. 196-281.

Notes to Chapter 4

1. See Martin Buber, *The Kingship of God*, translated by Richard Scheimann (New York: Harper Torchbooks, 1967); and Eric Voegelin, *Order and History*, vol. 1: *Israel and Revelation* (Baton Rouge: Louisiana State University Press, 1956), pp. 185-352. In addition to the biblical passages cited below, also note Psalm 47.
2. See Eric Voegelin, *Order and History*, Vol. 3: *Plato and Aristotle* (Baton Rouge: Louisiana State University Press, 1957).
3. See Victor Ehrenbert, *The Greek State* (New York: W.W. Norton, 1960), pp. 103-131.
4. Voegelin, Order and History, vol. 4: *The Ecumenic Age* (Baton Rouge: Louisiana State University Press, 1974), p. 226.
5. *Ibid.*, p. 227.

6. F. Parkinson, *The Philosophy of International Relations* (Beverly Hills: Sage Publications, 1977) [Sage Library of Social Research, Vol. 52], p. 10.
7. *Ibid.*, p. 11.
8. *Ibid.*, p. 12.
9. Cicero, *On the Commonwealth (De re Publica)*, translated by George H. Sabine and Stanley B. Smith (Indianapolis: The Bobbs-Merrill Co., 1976), p. 216 [Bk. III, 22].
10. Voegelin, *Ecumenic Age*, p. 47.
11. *Ibid.*
12. Parkinson, *Philosophy of International Relations*, p. 13.
13. *Ibid.*
14. See Herbert A. Deane, *The Political and Social Ideas of St. Augustine* (New York: Columbia University Press, 1963), pp. 78 ff.
15. *Ibid.*, p. 86.
16. *Ibid.*, pp. 116 ff.
17. *Ibid.*, pp. 97, 102.
18. *Ibid.*, p. 200.
19. *Ibid.*
20. From A.P. D'Entrèves, "Introduction," *Aquinas: Selected Political Writings*, edited by D'Entrèves, translated by J.G. Dawson (Oxford: Basil Blackwell, 1970), p. xxv.
21. Quoted in *Ibid.*, p. xxiii.

Notes to Chapter 5

1. Hans J. Morgenthau, *Truth and Power* (New York: Praeger, 1970).
2. *Ibid.*, p. 61.
3. *Ibid.*, pp. 62-63.
4. *Ibid.*, pp. 63-64.
5. As for the limits and problems involved in this assumption that the "depraved" condition of human nature explains international politics, see Kenneth Waltz, *Man, the State, and War*, pp. 16-41.
6. Morgenthau, *Truth and Power*, pp. 64-65.
7. Dougherty and Pfaltzgraff comment that the concept of the power struggle "gives continuity and unity to the seemingly

diverse foreign policies of the widely separated nation-states. Moreover, the concept 'interest defined as power' makes evaluating the actions of political leaders at different points in history possible.'' In other words, Morgenthau's attempt to define the universal uniformity of human nature provides him with the principle of universality and unity that is necessary without which the diversity would have no meaning or common relatinship. *Contending Theories of International Relations*, p. 76.

8. Morgenthau, "The Limits of Historical Justice," *Truth and Power*, p. 80.

9. *Ibid*.

10. Commenting on Hobbes, Eric Voegelin puts it beautifully: "The style of the construction is magnificent. If human nature is assumed to be nothing but passionate existence, devoid of ordering resources of the soul, the horror of annihilation will, indeed, be the overriding passion that compels submission to order. If pride cannot bow to Dike, or be redeemed through grace, it must be broken by the Leviathan who 'is king of all the children of pride.' If the souls cannot participate in the Logos, then the sovereign who strikes terror into the souls will be 'the essence of the commonwealth.' The 'King of the Proud' must break the *amor sui* that cannot be relieved by the *amor Dei*." *The New Science of Politics* (Chicago: University of Chicago Press, 1952), p. 184. Further on this theme of Morgenthau and Hobbes, see Cecil V. Crabb, Jr. and June Savoy, "Hans J. Morgenthau's Version of *Realpolitik*," *The Political Science Reviewer*, vol. 5 (Fall, 1975), pp. 201 ff., and 210 ff.

11. Morgenthau, "The Intellectual and Political Functions of Theory," *Truth and Power*, p. 252.

12. Morgenthau, "Common Sense and Theories," *Truth and Power*, pp. 242-243. The type of theory that Morgenthau is criticizing is the kind that attempts to reduce politics to some functional interrelationship such as economic, or the kind that is attempting to reduce international relations to quantifiable units that can yield greater predictability.

13. *Ibid*., p. 243.

14. Morgenthau, "The Intellectual and Political Functions of Theory," *Truth and Power*, p. 257.

15. *Ibid*., pp. 256-7. For more on Morgenthau's conception of

political theory as rational hypotheses testing, see his *Politics Among Nations* (New York: Knopf, 1967), pp. 4 ff. (4th edition).

16. "The Intellectual and Political Functions of Theory," *Truth and Power*, p. 257.

17. Crabb and Savoy comment, "Why the intellectuals within a society escape involvement in the 'universal' power struggle—or why the moral-ethical professions of intellectuals do not also conceal an egocentric quest for power—are questions Morgenthau never clarifies," "Hans J. Morgenthau's Version of *Realpolitik*," p. 202.

18. "The Intellectual and Political Functions of Theory," pp. 259-260.

19. *Ibid.*, pp. 260-261.

20. Deutsch, *The Analysis of International Relations*, 2nd edition (Englewood Cliffs, N.J.: Prentice-Hall, 1978), p. 91.

21. *Ibid.*

22. *Ibid.*, pp. 89-90. Another example is Deutsch's comparison of the political system with a telephone switchboard. See his *The Nerves of Government* (New York: The Free Press, 1964), pp. 76-98. In this latter book Deutsch develops his basic cybernetic-systems theory that underlies all of his policital analysis.

23. Deutsch's book is amazing in its total lack of historical accounting even of its own assumptions. The following statement that introduces Chapter Two on the "Tools for Thinking" is utterly nominalistic in character, but Deutsch nowhere indicates that he is even aware of this. "Since a concept is a symbol, and a symbol is, so to speak, a command to be mindful of those things to which it refers, it follows that a concept is a kind of command to remember a collection of things or memories. It is an order to select and collect certain items of information—these will refer to facts, *if* they should happen to exist. Hence a concept is a command to search, but it is no guarantee that we shall find." *Analysis of International Relations*, p. 14. See also the beginning of Chapter Four, p. 45, for a similar comment.

24. *Ibid.*, p. 9.

25. *Ibid.*, p. 10.

26. See especially Deutsch's *The Nerves of Government*. Also note Robert L. Pfaltzgraff, Jr., "Karl Deutsch and the Study of

Political Science," *The Political Science Reviewer*, vol. 2 (Fall, 1972), pp. 90-111.

27. *Analysis of International Relations*, p. 14.
28. When Deutsch, both in this book and elsewhere defines a "people," he does so in a very abstract way: "A people, then, is a group with complementary communication habits whose members usually share the same language, and always share a similar culture so that all members of the group attach the same meanings to words. In that sense a people is a community of shared meanings." *Politics and Government: How People Decide Their Fate*, 2nd edition (Boston: Houghton Mifflin Co., 1974), p. 130. A *state* or political system, for Deutsch, pre-supposes one or more *peoples*, and it is then defined (also quite abstractly) as "an organization for the enforcement of decisions or commands, made practicable by the existing habits of compliance among the population . . . A state can be used to reinforce the communication habits, the cooperation, and the solidarity of people." *Analysis of International Relations*, p. 79.
29. The term "nation-state" which Deutsch frequently uses manifests one of the ways in which he has inadequately identified politics or the state or a political system. Note especially the criticism of Walker Connor, "Nation-Building or Nation-Destroying," *World Politics*, vol. 24 (April, 1972), pp. 319-355.
30. *Analysis of International Relations*, p. 19.
31. *Ibid.*, p. 198.
32. *Ibid.*, p. 224.
33. *Ibid.*, pp. 224-225.
34. *Ibid.*, p. 253.
35. Pfaltzgraff comments: "Deutsch calls for unprecedented breakthroughs in the social sciences toward an understanding of international conflict. His assumption is that, having gained such understanding, peoples would forego war for peace. He thus calls for a transformation in human behavior as remarkable as the advances which he proposes in the social sciences. The political transformation for which Deutsch calls at the international level far exceeds both in scope and in rapidity those which he describes in the development historically of political communities at the national level. If the prospects for

their realization in the international system of the next generation are minimal, the question remains as to whether Deutsch's assessment of the future is accurate." "Karl Deutsch and the Study of Political Science," p. 107. For some background and criticism of the traditions in which Deutsch stands, see Floyd W. Matson, *The Broken Image* (Garden City: Doubleday Anchor Books, 1964), Chapter Three, "The Manipulated Society: Politics as the Science of Behavior," pp. 66-110; Alec Barbrook, *Patterns of Political Behavior* (Itasca, Ill.: F.E. Peacock, 1975); Stanislav Andreski, *Social Sciences as Sorcery* (New York: St. Martin's Press, 1972); Gabriel Almond, "Political Theory and Political Science," *American Political Science Review*, vol. 60 (December, 1966), pp. 869-879; Robert A. Dahl, "The Behavioral Approach in Political Science," in Nelson W. Polsby, Robert A. Dentler, and Paul A. Smith, editors, *Politics and Social Life* (Boston: Houghton Mifflin Co., 1963); Peter Nettl, "Concept of System in Political Science," *Political Studies* (October, 1966), pp. 305-338.

36. At thus juncture, however, Keohane and Nye refer specifically to Robert Angell, *Peace on the March: Transnational Participation* (New York: Van Nostrand, 1969).

37. Keohane and Nye, *Power and Interdependence* (Boston: Little, Brown, and Co., 1977), p. 4.

38. Keohane and Nye argue that three assumptions are integral to the realist vision: "First, states as coherent units are the dominant actors in world politics . . . Second, realists assume that force is a usable and effective instrument of policy . . . Third, partly because of their second assumption, realists assume a hierarchy of issues in world politics, headed by questions of military security: the 'high politics' of military security dominates the 'low politics' of economic and social affairs." *Ibid.*, pp. 23-24.

39. *Ibid.*, pp. 18-19.

40. *Ibid.*, p. 162.

41. *Ibid.*, p. 224.

42. *Ibid.*, p. 221. On this subject, as well as on some others, see the following works produced by Keohane and Nye: "Transgovernmental Relations and International Organizations," *World Politics*, vol. 27 (October, 1974), pp. 39-62; "International Interdependence and Integration," in Fred I. Greenstein and

Nelson W. Polsby (eds.), *Handbook of Political Science*, vol. 8 (Reading, Mass.: Addison-Wesley, 1975), pp. 363-414; and as editors, *Transnational Relations and World Politics* (Cambridge, Mass.: Harvard University Press, 1972).

Notes to Chapter 6

1. See for example, Walter Laqueur and Barry Rubin, *The Human Rights Reader* (New York: Meridian Books, 1979).
2. Some recent publications are worthy of note: Jack L. Nelson and Vera M. Green, *International Human Rights: Contemporary Issues* (Pine Plains, N.Y.: Human Rights Publishing Group, 1980); Asbjørn Eide, *Human rights in the World Society* (Pine Plains, N.Y.: Human Rights Publishing Group, 1980); Allen O. Miller, *Christian Declaration on Human Rights* (Grand Rapids, Mich.: Eerdmans Publishing Co., 1977); David Owen, *Human Rights* (New York: W.W. Norton, 1978); J.D. Van der Vyver, *Seven Lectures on Human Rights* (Cape Town: Juta and Co., 1976); C.F. Forsyth and J.E. Schiller, eds., *Human Rights: The Cape Town Conference* (1979) (Cape Town: Juta and Co., 1979).
3. Buckley, "Human Rights and Foreign Policy: A Proposal," *Foreign Affairs*, vol. 58, no. 4 (Spring, 1980), p. 785.
4. *Ibid.*, p. 793.
5. See Arthur Schlesinger, Jr., "Human Rights and the American Tradition," *Foreign Affairs*, vol. 57, no. 3 (1979), pp. 503-526; Sandy Vogelgesang, *American Dream Global Nightmare: The Dilemma of U.S. Human Rights Policy* (New York: W.W. Norton, 1980); Leo J. Wollenborg, "Human Rights and Carter's Policy," *Worldview* (October, 1978), pp. 12-15.
6. A good article that uncovers part of this problem is Rupert Emerson, "The New Higher Law of Anti-Colonialism," in Karl Deutsch and Stanley Hoffmann, eds., *The Relevance of International Law* (Garden City, N.Y.: Doubleday Anchor Books, 1971), pp. 203-230. Also see Gary D. Glenn, "Inalienable Rights and Positive Government in the Modern World," *Journal of Politics*, vol. 41 (1979), pp. 1057 ff.; and the Dutch work (with English summary) by G.J. Veerman, *Het zelfbeschikkingsrecht der naties en de rechten van de mens* [The Self-Deter-

mination of Nations and Human Rights] (Amsterdam: Academische Pers, 1977).

7. Note David Luban's "Just War and Human Rights," *Philosophy and Public Affairs*, vol. 9, no. 2 (Winter, 1980), pp. 160-181.

8. See, for example, G. Feaver, "Wounded Knee and the New Tribalism," *Encounter*, vol. 44 (1975), Feb., pp. 28-35; March, pp. 16-24; April, pp. 33-46; May, pp. 23-34; Paul Marshall, "The Basis of Human Rights in Canada," *The Guide* (Organ of the Christian Labour Association of Canada), vol. 28, no. 5 (June/July, 1980), pp. 10-12; and Walker Connor, "Nation-Building and Nation-Destroying," *World Politics* (April, 1972), pp. 319-355.

9. James W. Skillen, "Justice for Representation," a pamphlet published by the Association for Public Justice, Box 56348, Washington, D.C. 20011.

10. On the matter of diverse perspectives, cultures, and antagonisms relating to human rights and international law, see Mohammed Bedjaoui, *Towards a New International Economic Order* (New York: Holmes and Meier, 1980); Adamantia Pollis and Peter Schwab, eds., *Human Rights: Cultural and Ideological Perspectives* (New York: Praeger Publishers, 1979); and Raul S. Manglapus, "Human Rights are Not a Western Discovery," *Worldview* (October, 1978), pp. 4-6.

11. For some background here see: Herman Dooyeweerd, "What is Man?", Chapter 8 in his *In the Twilight of Western Thought* (Nutley, N.J.: The Craig Press, 1968), and Dooyeweerd, *Roots of Western Culture*, translated by John Kraay, and edited by Mark Vander Vennen and Bernard Zylstra (Toronto: Wedge Publishing Foundation, 1979); James W. Skillen, *Christians Organizing for Political Service* (Washington, D.C.: APJ Education Fund, 1980); and Bob Goudzwaard, *A Christian Political Option*, translated by Herman Praamsma (Toronto: Wedge Publishing Foundation, 1972).

12. Consider, for example, the fine paper by Bob Goudzwaard and John van Baars, "Norms for the International Economic Order," in *Justice in the International Economic Order*, Proceedings of the Second International Conference of Reformed Institutions for Higher Education (Grand Rapids, Mich.: Calvin College, 1980), pp. 223-253; D.D. Raphael, ed., *Politi-*

cal Theory and the Rights of Man (Bloomington: Indiana University Press, 1967); and Herman Dooyeweerd, *The Christian Idea of the State* (Nutley, N.J.: The Craig Press, 1968).
13. James W. Skillen, "Problems of Theory in Political Integration: Europe," *Philosophia Reformata*, 40th Year (1975), pp. 141-159.

Notes to Chapter 7

1. Macpherson, *The Political Theory of Possessive Individualism* (New York: Oxford University Press, 1962).
2. Grondona, "From Empire to Imperialism: The United States in the Midst of Change," in *A Nation Observed: Perspectives on America's World Role*, Donald R. Lesh, ed. (Washington, D.C.: Potomac Associates, 1974), p. 93.
3. Fagan, "The United States and Chile: Roots and Branches," *Foreign Affairs*, vol. 53 (January, 1975), pp. 310-311.
4. "The New Higher Law of Anti-Colonialism," in *The Relevance of International Law*, Karl Deutsch and Stanley Hoffmann, eds. (Garden City: Doubleday Anchor Books, 1971), p. 214.
5. Jacques Ellul, *The Political Illusion*, translated by Konrad Kellen (New York: Vintage Books, 1967), p. 9.
6. Fagan, "The United States and Chile," pp. 312-313.
7. Los Angeles speech, January 24, 1975.